The Phrasal Verb in English

Le Merton

DWIGHT BOLINGER

The Phrasal Verb in English

Harvard University Press, Cambridge, Massachusetts 1971

Distributed in Great Britain
by Oxford University Press, London

Library of Congress Catalog Card Number 73-150011

SBN 674-66625-9

Printed in the United States of America

To the memory of Peter Erades

Acknowledgments

The debt to my predecessors is obvious on every page, and I can only offer the flattery of imitation as my inadequate thanks. But two persons who went out of their way to be helpful deserve a more explicit expression of gratitude: Bruce Fraser, who allowed me to study his unpublished book on phrasal verbs, and J. P. Maher, who brought Dimiter Spasov's work to my attention.

For their hospitality and assistance in gathering some of the material for this volume, I thank the staff of the English Language Survey of University College, London, and its director, Randolph Quirk. For the means to finish it, I thank the American Philosophical Society and its Penrose Fund, the Guggenheim Memorial Foundation, and the Center for Advanced Study in the Behavioral Sciences.

Contents

Foreword

Every language provides a means to coin out of its own substance. English has been thought to be rather impoverished in this regard. Statistics are quoted on vast importations from French and more or less artificial graftings from Greek and Latin. For the linguist trained on written texts, who listens with only half an ear, these chiseled borrowings obscure an outpouring of lexical creativeness that surpasses anything else in our language. We call it the phrasal verb: *to help out, to write up, to die off, to string along, to gad about.*

Of such combinations of verb and particle Old English had only a trace. The adverb appeared instead more commonly before the verb, whether conjoined or not. The number grew slowly in the Middle English period, then received a setback, at least in the literary language, from the influx of Romance derivatives and did not get going strongly again until the fifteenth century. Numerous virtual doublets show the competition: pairs like *blow out* and *extinguish, come in* and *enter, get around* and *circumvent.*[1] But it is now quite unequal. Many

1. Paraphrased from Kennedy, pp. 12–14, 31–32. In a study based on forty-six plays from the early Renaissance to the present, Spasov finds the phrasal verb at lowest ebb in the second half of the eighteenth century—probably because of fashions in writing. His graph (p. 21) showing percentages of phrasal verbs in the total of verbs counted for each of the eight periods he distinguishes, follows:

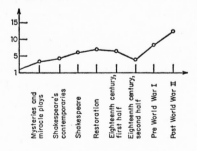

Latinate forms have themselves picked up "redundant" particles: we would not feel comfortable now without the *through* in *With a little pressure the needle finally perforated through.* And forms like *extend out, refer back,* and *proceed forth* are common, though some, such as *retrieve back, extract out,* and *include in* may be regarded as nonstandard. Furthermore the phrasal verb probably accounts for more new "stereotypes" than any other source. I must use this term rather than "new words" because of our typewriter-space notions of what words are. I mean by it a lexical unit in the strict sense of a nonadditive compound or derivative, one that has a set meaning which is not the sum of the meanings of its parts.

Why the success? It must lie in the familiarity and manageability of the elements. The vast majority of the source verbs are common Germanic monosyllables, and the particles are a limited number of highly frequent adverbs and prepositions, with an occasional adjective. Moreover, they are *words.* The everyday inventor is not required to reach for elements such as roots and affixes that have no reality for him. It takes only a rough familiarity with other uses of *head* and *off* to make them available for *head off,* virtually self-suggesting when the occasion for them comes up, which is not true of learnèd formations like *intercept.* So we get *to luck up, to goof off, to psych out.*

It also lies in imagery. The phrasal verb is a floodgate of metaphor. Words from other sources are apt to be sharply differentiated—one does not nowadays think of the verb *to insult* as being once a literal equivalent of *to jump on;* and similarly *to exult* "to jump up and down with joy" and *to assault* "to jump at" come sealed in tight capsules of meaning. But with the phrasal verb this contact with original metaphor is maintained and gives rise to extensions that are as colorful as they are numerous. Take the phrasal verb *to step out.* In all its meanings the metaphorical core lies bare, though of course we are free to ignore it:

I'm stepping out for a few minutes. (absenting myself)
We're stepping out tonight. (celebrating)
She's stepping out on him. (two-timing him)

The phrasal verb shares with all compounds, but magnified because of the freedom of its elements, the advantage of being "always motivated and hence strikingly expressive."[2]

Beyond and contributing to its own success, is that of its progeny in another sphere. The phrasal verb is—next to noun + noun combinations—probably the most prolific source of new nouns in English.[3] It generates them by the same stress-shift rule that gives us *ímport* from *impórt*, *dígest* from *digést*, *cómbine* from *combíne*, and so forth; hence *stándoff* from *stand óff*, *rúnaway* from *run awáy*, *mákeup* from *make úp*, *gét together* from *get togéther*. Here we acquire many of our names for the kaleidoscope of contemporary social phenomena: *sit-in*, *wade-in*, *love-in*, *dropout*, *lockout*, *fallout*, *cook-out*, *freakout*, *hangup*, *spin-off*.

The familiarity of the forms, their relative fluidity and the feeling that these are not really "individual words," and the way dictionaries are put together conspire against giving due credit to phrasal verbs as a chapter of generative morphology. Most of them are usually listed as subentries under the verb proper, even though the semantic subordination may be slight or nonexistent, and the result is that they are not counted— much as if *disease* were listed under *ease* and *mistake* under *take*. And their semantic complexity is thereby slighted. *Webster's Third New International* enters *to play off* in one

2. Jose Joaquín Montes in *Thesaurus* (*Boletín del Instituto Caro y Cuervo*) 23:32 (1968).

3. Not counting as new nouns the mere changes of meaning in "old" nouns.

(not all) of its senses under *to play,* and defines it as "to set in opposition."[4] If it were merely this, it could be used like *to match: *The promoters played off the challenger against the champion.* What *play off* means, more precisely, is "set (two sides) in opposition so as to avoid harm (from either)." Oversimplified definitions are an encouragement to simplistic treatments of semantics. In some cases the phrasal verb is not recognized at all except by examples of some general definition. Thus the phrasal verb *to bring to light* is not recorded by *Webster's Third New International* but there is a special definition of *light,* which is "open view, public knowledge," illustrated by an example with *bring.* This is misleading because it suggests the possibility of *withdraw from light* for "conceal" or *the light was poor* for "the public was ignorant," whereas *light* with this meaning has no function outside that one phrasal verb—we cannot even say **expose to light* or **hold to light.* All in all, the published records by which we judge the intricacy of our lexicon and which condition our thinking about it play us false and tempt us to notions about the analyzability of morphemes—and the size of the lexicon as a whole—that are quite unrealistic. The amount of language that comes ready made is vastly greater than supposed, and phrasal verbs are only one of the more regular, more easily described, zones of neglect.

In this book I do not attempt to remedy the lack of an inventory of phrasal verbs nor to examine more than incidentally the problem of how they are generated and what relationships they have with simple verbs. I am concerned instead with syntactic questions: component categories, possibilities of arrangement, the effects of context, and the tension between stereotyping and dynamics. Among these questions is one

---

4. Though I cite this, I excuse myself from the company of those who bait that fine dictionary.

whose answer must be added to the guarantees of success that I have already mentioned: how phrasal verbs interact with the prosody of English sentences.

It is customary to apologize for serving as one's own informant. No apology is necessary if the intent is to explore as inventively as possible what *can* be done with a construction. A fair scattergram of the possibilities can be got by examining just what has been written or heard, but the critical cases often lie an inch or two beyond. We cannot know what our language allows us to do until we stretch it to its limits, and that is only done by children and introspective linguists; everyday speakers stay comfortably most of the time in the well-furnished interior. Being one's own informant is like being a composer. One listens for hints and then invents and judges for fitness at the same time, expecting that others will resonate.

The reader will decide whether my musical composition has been successful. He is bound to find fault with some of the harmonies, but I ask him then to weigh them in terms of better or worse rather than right or wrong. When I declare *A* to be acceptable and *B* not, I can usually be satisfied if he finds *A* unacceptable but *B* more so. We differ then in the precise location of the boundary, but not in its relationship to the whole.

Works on the phrasal verb, or treating it *in extenso,* which are cited by page or section reference only

Erades, Peter. "Points of Modern English Syntax, XL." *English Studies* 42:56-60 (1961).

Fairclough, Norman L. "Some English Phrasal Types: Studies in the Collocation of Lexical Items with Prepositions and Adverbs in a Corpus of Spoken and Written Present-day English." M.A. thesis, University College London, 1965.

Fraser, Bruce. "The Verb-Particle Construction in English." Unpub. ms.

Hill, L. A. *Prepositions and Adverbial Particles: An Interim Classification, Semantic, Structural, and Graded.* London, Oxford University Press, 1968.

Jespersen, Otto. *A Modern English Grammar on Historical Principles.* Vol. III. London, George Allen and Unwin, Ltd. 1928.

Kennedy, Arthur G. *The Modern English Verb-Adverb Combination.* Stanford University Publications in Language and Literature. Vol. I, no. 1. Stanford, California, 1920.

Konishi, Tomshichi. "The Growth of the Verb-Adverb Combination in English: A Brief Sketch," in Kazua Araki et al., eds., *Studies in English Grammar and Linguistics: A Miscellany in Honour of Takanobu Otsuka.* Tokyo, Kenkyusha, 1958.

Kruisinga, E. *A Handbook of Present-day English.* Part II, *English Accidence and Syntax.* 5th ed. Groningen, P. Noordhoff, 1931–32.

Live, Anna H. "The Discontinuous Verb in English," *Word* 21:428–451 (1965).

Meyer, George A. Unpub. paper on phrasal verbs.

Mitchell, T. F. "Syntagmatic Relations in Linguistic Analysis," *Transactions of the Philological Society* (1958), pp. 101–118.

Palmer, F. R. *A Linguistic Study of the English Verb.* London, Longmans, Green and Co., 1965.

Poutsma, H. *A Grammar of Late Modern English.* (Unless otherwise noted, all references are to Part I, "The Sentence," First Half) 2nd ed. Groningen, P. Noordhoff, 1928.

Spasov, Dimiter. *English Phrasal Verbs.* Sofia, Naouka i Izkoustvo, 1966.

Taha, Abdul Karim. "The Structure of Two-Word Verbs in English," *Language Learning* 10:115–122 (1960).

van Dongen, W. A., Sr. *"He put on his hat* and *He put his hat on."* *Neophilologus: A Modern Language Quarterly* (Groningen) 4:322–353 (1919).

The Phrasal Verb in English

CHAPTER 1

Terms and Coverage

I adopt the term phrasal verb purely for convenience, as the one most generally accepted.[1] Others would serve just as well: Abdul Taha's "two-word verb," Anna Live's "discontinuous verb," E. Kruisinga's "compound verb" (§§2204–2211), Bruce Fraser's "verb-particle construction," or Arthur Kennedy's tentative "verb-adverb compound," which he suggested (p. 9) and then put aside. Kennedy was unwilling to accept anything that implied a commitment as to how close a connection there must be in order to have a compound. He sensed all degrees of connectedness, from tightly bound phrases like *put out* in *put out a fire* through more loosely connected ones like *blot out* in *blot out the mistake* to others that are barely federated, like *brush out* in *brush out the dirt*—and the latter extreme, he said (p. 9), "shades off imperceptibly into the great mass of adverbial modifications such as *fly away, walk south, go home,* etc." It is enough that "phrasal verb" avoids this commitment, does not exclude phrases of more than two words (as "two-word verb" does), and is comfortable.

Obviously not all phrases containing verbs are phrasal verbs. We are interested in combinations about which generalizations can be made—which display shared regularities or irregularities and show some special degree of cohesion that sets them apart

---

1. It is used by Dimiter Spasov, M. A. K. Halliday ("Class in Relation to the Axes of Chain and Choice," *Linguistics* 2:11 [1963]), F. R. Palmer, Norman Fairclough, W. H. Mittins (according to Fairclough), and Logan Pearsall Smith, who attributes it (I owe this reference also to Fairclough, p. 50) to Henry Bradley. Smith writes: "The term 'phrasal verbs' was suggested to me by the late Dr. Bradley; not, as he wrote, that he was satisfied with it." (*Words and Idioms: Studies in the English Language* [London, Constable and Co., Ltd., 1933], p. 172.)

from the more freely composable constructions like *to fall headlong, to live at home,* or *to leave tomorrow.* Within this roughly narrowed field it would be possible to treat a number of rather distinct clusters, and those who have dealt with the subject have differed on what they preferred to include. All have agreed on the most central forms: they consist of a verb proper and an adverbial particle such as *up, out,* or *over,* though not necessarily all instances of even these three have been accorded equal status. Peripheral clusters have been described and either defined into the class of phrasal verbs or defined out of it. To keep my discussion within limits I follow suit and exclude the following:

1. The type which includes *to rely on, to rail at, to cope with, to confide in, to feel like* (*crying*), and *to dote on.* As will be shown later, the particle in these combinations is pure preposition; this reduces their syntactic flexibility, leaving them almost as rigid as one-word verbs:

I can cope with Jones, all right.

I can manage Jones, all right.

*I can cope Jones with, all right.

It also reduces the accentual flexibility which will be the theme of a later section; in

He can be relíed on.

He can be trústed.

the possibility of accenting *on* is slight, whereas in

It needs to be held úp.

It needs to be héld up.

the speaker chooses according to his meaning.[2] All such com-

---

2. In one small respect there is more freedom than with one-word verbs, for example,

He's a person I would never dare ráil át!

He's a person I would never dare scóld!

Here the extra syllable, though normally unaccented, can be accented; this point is treated at the end of Chapter 3. But the pure preposition is no match for the adverb in this respect.

binations are stereotyped and highly idiomatic. They readily include nouns (*to give rise to, to be a match for*), adjectives (*to be fond of, to make free with, to steer clear of*), and adverbial particles (*to put up with, to be up to, to look down on*). The result is that no large-scale gradient can be traced between more or less freely composable phrases through degrees of figurative extension down to more or less tightly bound stereotypes with the steps clearly interrelatable and often systematic and predictable—as can be done with what I choose to regard as phrasal verbs proper. The phrases with pure prepositions are more accidental and contribute relatively little to the expansive power of English.[3] The following classification by Mitchell (p. 106) makes the necessary distinctions:

nonphrasal	{ nonprepositional, *to take*
	{ prepositional, *to take to*
phrasal	{ nonprepositional, *to put up*
	{ prepositional, *to put up with*

Our interest here is in the phrasal nonprepositional type.

2. In general, combinations of verb with complement other than an adverbial particle, though a few must be admitted because of their close resemblance to verb-particle combinations. So I exclude, as Fraser does (p. 55), such phrases as *to fall ill, to ring true, to loom large, to sit tight, to blow hot and cold, to die happy, to eat crow, to turn turtle, to cut a figure, to do nicely, to wish well, to pay handsomely,*

3. Both Fairclough and Fraser treat them in detail. Fraser discusses (pp. 58–68) the restrictions on such types as *make reference to, set eyes on, take (something) in stride,* and *cast anchor.* Fairclough (p. 52) classifies according to the number and order of elements, for example, SVCPPN: *Let's cast our minds back to the day;* SVPCPN: *throw in their lot with the Socialists;* SVPPN: *His master lives up to such service,* and so on; his observations are especially useful (chap. 4) for showing gradience in the tie between verb and preposition, for example, *look after* versus *stay at.* L. A. Hill shows gradience also, with a notation for several degrees of connectedness.

to go to bed, to go to sleep, and the like. It is no embarrassment that I must later qualify this exclusion, for I do not believe that a linguistic entity such as the phrasal verb can be confined within clear bounds. Rather there are analogical extensions in all directions, some of which along with their causes and effects must be traced; being or not being a phrasal verb is a matter of degree.

If the phrasal verb is such as entity as I have described, it ought to be amenable to the multiple-criteria treatment devised by the Survey of English Usage.[4] So it would appear to be; but the job has been done in piecemeal fashion: each investigator has had one or two pet criteria, but no one has attempted to tabulate the response of even a sample of phrasal verbs to the full set of criteria if all were added together. Nor will I attempt it, for reasons I hope to make clear; but this is the appropriate place to list the tests that have been applied.

1. The most general of all is replaceability by a simple verb. Live (p. 428) compares *count out* to *exclude, look into* to *investigate, egg on* to *incite, get around* to *circumvent,* and so on. This includes both too little and too much. Many obvious candidates cannot be matched with items from the more meager stock of learnèd words:

The plane took off. ("departed" is not specific)

He broke out with a rash. ("erupted" is ludicrous)

He hauled off and hit me. (no synonym that I am aware of, unless we admit "He upped and hit me")

We would not want to leave these out, nor would we want to include any such string as *to eat dinner, to make a mistake,* or *to impose restraint upon or limit in motion or action* because they can be replaced by *to dine, to err,* and *to hold* respectively.

4. See H. T. Carvell and Jan Svartvik, *Computational Experiments in Grammatical Classification* (The Hague, Mouton and Co., 1969).

2. If transitive, the combination should passivize. This test has some limited usefulness in combinations with pure prepositions, to determine which are stereotyped and which are not:

They talked about you → You were talked about.

The house stands near the lake ↛ *The lake is stood near by the house.

But with the mixed adverb and preposition (adprep) that will be explained in the next chapter, it is useless. It would, for example, allow in virtually all combinations with *go* but exclude virtually also those with *come:*

He went into the subject carefully → The subject was gone into carefully.

He came into a fortune → *A fortune was come into.

We have gone across that lake so many times that no guide is necessary → That lake has been gone across so many times . . .

We have come across that lake so many times . . . ↛ *That lake has been come across so many times . . .

I came across the money I had lost ↛ *The money was come across.

(*To come by* is the only exception that occurs to me:

He came by a fortune → A fortune is not easily come by.)

For the typical phrasal verbs that are the burden of this study, the test hardly does more than confirm transitivity, which is not likely to be in doubt. Thus *to stare* is intransitive and *to stare down* is transitive, which makes transitivity per se in such parallel cases an indication of being a phrasal verb, whence

They stared the man down → The man was stared down.

If the verb proper is already transitive but does not itself passivize, failure to passivize does not exclude the combination from the class of phrasal verbs. So for *have* and *have in* "entertain":

We had in some friends → *Some friends were had in.[5]

3. If transitive, the combination should yield an action nominal. This was proposed by R. B. Lees[6] and applied by Fairclough (p. 16) and Fraser (p. 3 and passim). Thus for *look into* and *look up:*

> He looked up the information → His looking up of the information.

> He looked into the information ↛ *His looking into of the information.

This is a useful test for culling out pure prepositions, but with the mixed prepositions (adpreps) it yields contradictory results. Thus it would appear that *to run up the hill* and *to walk across the bridge* are parallel in every respect, yet

> The running up of the hill was a matter of minutes.

> *The walking across of the bridge was a matter of minutes.

Similarly with *They drilled through the hardpan* and *They broke through the screen:*

> The drilling through of the hardpan was easy.

> *The breaking through of the screen was easy.

It appears that the nature of the actions rather than the structure of the phrases is what determines at least these particular

5. Live proposes this test, but it fails to exclude what she wants excluded. Her starred *The stage was acted on* and *The stairs were run up* (p. 435) are normal, given a little context: *This stage has never been acted on before; These stairs have been run up so many times that the carpet is in shreds.* Fraser also proposes it (p. 87) to exclude *on* meaning "continuation" from the class of particles that can form phrasal verbs. Thus *to babble on about* presumably does not passivize:

* The campaign was babbled on about.

But this restriction applies more to the motivation for a particular passive than to the grammar of phrasal verbs. One can imagine an impatient listener saying

This campaign has been babbled on and on about just too, too long.

The point is unimportant except to illustrate the general unreliability of passivization.

6. *A Grammar of English Nominalizations* (The Hague, Mouton and Co., 1963), p. 22.

nominals: we can topicalize the running up of hills and the drilling through of hardpan because those are things that "get done to" hills and hardpan by racers and drillers; we do not think of walking across and breaking through as concerted actions that "get done to" bridges and screens. Compare:

Look at your map and check the progress of the runners; Hill No. 2 has obviously been run up already.

. . . *the bridge has obviously been walked across already.

Look at the hole here—the hardpan has obviously been drilled through already.

. . . ?the screen has obviously been broken through already.

—this in spite of the fact that all the constructions involved readily passivize.

A corollary of the action nominal test has been used to distinguish between verb + adverb combinations that are not entitled to be regarded as phrasal verbs, and verb + adverb-particle combinations that are so entitled. The latter supposedly do not permit the particle to be placed after the direct object. The following examples are Fraser's (p. 3):

His throwing up of his dinner was stupid.

*His throwing of his dinner up was stupid.

His throwing up of the ball was stupid.

His throwing of the ball up (rather than down) was stupid.

The effect of separating the verb and the particle in this fashion is to literalize both. A highly idiomatic phrasal verb such as *throw up,* in which both *throw* and *up* have deviated semantically from their meanings as separate items, does not admit the separation. But in between we can find many combinations which by most accounts we would want to regard as phrasal verbs which do admit it provided the verb more or less retains its literal sense and the particle is not made conspicuous. The effect of conspicuousness—particularly being placed in position to receive the terminal accent while other elements (specifically the direct object) are deprived of it—is to signal literalness. Take the three combinations *to yield up, to hand over,* and *to walk through.* With bare terminal position following a noun direct object, the result is bad:

    *The yielding of the key of the city up.

    *The handing of the merchandise over.

    *The walking of the papers through.

Yet the first two are normal if the accent-expecting noun is replaced by a personal pronoun:

    The yielding of it up.

    The handing of it over.

And the second and third are normal if the sentence is arranged to defuse the particle:

    The handing of anything over that has so much value must
        be attended by proper safeguards.

    The walking of such papers through at that hour—almost
        five o'clock—was an imposition on the clerical staff.

The particle *up* gives trouble in phrase-terminal position even when highly literal, which probably accounts for the difficulty with *yield up;* so for the literal *move up* and *move down:*

    His moving of the lever down was ill-advised.

    ?His moving of the lever up was ill-advised.

At best, this corollary to the action nominal test serves to separate two extremes of the gradient of phrasal verbs.

The next three tests (4, 5, and 6) are grouped together by Fairclough (p. 13) as his main criteria; he adopts them from Mitchell:

4. If the combination is transitive, the particle can either precede or follow the noun object. Thus:

    He looked up his friends.

    He looked his friends up.

    They bought out their competitors.

    They bought their competitors out.

This test serves to eliminate, as particles, pure adverbs on the one hand:

*He sold regretfully the business.

He sold the business regretfully.

and prepositions on the other:

I stood in the doorway.

*I stood the doorway in.

But it leaves an area of doubt with certain adpreps:

I walked over the hill.

?I walked the hill over.

I walked that hill all over from top to bottom without find-
    ing a trace of the ring I had lost.

And it also needs to be used in conjunction with Test 8 below; this is to say that the nature of the object noun phrase makes a difference:

I would sell regretfully any business in which I had been
    engaged for half a lifetime.

But with this proviso, the test is reliable. Where it fails, the reasons are consistent with the same theory that explains its success.

5. If the combination is transitive, pronouns usually precede the particle:

How did you find that out?

?How did you find out that?

You're putting him on!

*You're putting on him!

Personal pronouns are a special case and will receive attention in Chapter 3. Despite the "usually" hedge, the test is useful because it is the easiest of all to make. But theoretical condi-tions are the same as with Test 4, and are discussed in Chapter 4.

6. Whether the combination is transitive or intransitive, ad-verbs cannot intervene between the verb and the particle unless

the latter appears in its most literal sense. To use Fraser's examples.

*The debater drew his opponent only part-way out.

The debater drew the lucky number only part-way out.

But this is like Test 3. It separates the extreme of independent adverbs from the extreme of bound adverb-particles. It will be useful in showing degrees of bondage (see Chapters 9 and 11), but it cannot be imposed as an absolute criterion. We would, for example, probably want to regard *to let out* in *to let out a seam* as a phrasal verb; but

She let the seam neatly out.

is a normal sentence.[7] The insertion of adverbs reacts to stereotyping even with obvious metaphors. If a metaphor is fresh, the adverb can be inserted. Thus *to push up* can be literally to exert pressure on a physical object or figuratively to do the same with an imagined "object":

Can't you push this side just a wee bit up?

Can't you push your estimate just a wee bit up?

But if the metaphor is second-hand, insertion is more difficult; so for *to drop out* in the academic sense, and *to climb down* referring to behavior:

I watched the pebbles drop gradually out.

7. Irrelevant considerations can enter in disguise, as in the following (from Fraser):
* The wind slowed completely down.
The man climbed completely down.
which reputedly shows *slow down* to be a phrasal verb while *climb down* is not. Yet we find *The engine slowed all the way down* and would hardly feel justified in saying that when the wind slows down we have a phrasal verb, but when an engine slows down we do not. The difference is a fact of the real world: there is a definite terminus to which an engine can slow down "all the way"—the point, say, where the foot is entirely removed from the throttle but a minimum of fuel is still passing through; but there is no such point for the wind short of stopping altogether; for the wind, "completely" (= stopping) and "slowing down" (= still going) are a contradiction in terms.

*I'm afraid you'll find these transfer students dropping gradually out.

I'm afraid you'll find these transfer students gradually dropping out.

He climbed grudgingly down from his horse and let me mount.

*He climbed grudgingly down from his high horse and started acting human.

He grudgingly climbed down from his high horse and started acting human.

The interpolation of adverbs makes a more interesting test for pure prepositions as against adpreps, as will be shown in Chapter 2:

He walked gaily with his two old chums whom he's not seen in years.

*He walked with gaily his two old chums . . .

He walked gaily up the first hill he came to.

He walked up gaily the first hill he came to.

7. An adverb can be accented.[8] This accent is applied in two ways, first to distinguish adverbs or adverb-particles from pure prepositions, and second, in the form of contrastive accent,

---

8. As I use the terms, stress and accent are properties of morphology and prosody respectively. In the word *Nimrod* the first syllable is stressed, and the dictionary entry will so mark it. Whether or not the word *Nimrod* is accented depends on the importance the speaker wishes to give it in an utterance. If it is repeated, for example in the answer of the following interchange,

Why didn't they call him Nimrod?—Because he didn't behave like a Nimrod.

it is not accented. If it is not accented the syllables *Nim-* and *-rod* have approximately equal prominence. But when it is accented the stressed syllable is the one that is made to stand out. Stress is thus the *potential* to receive the accent (and is predetermined at a fixed syllable in most English words), but accent is the privilege of the utterance. See Bolinger, "Contrastive accent and contrastive stress," *Language* 37.83–96 (1961).

to distinguish the first two, adverbs and adverb-particles, from each other.

It is true that prepositions, by and large, do not normally carry the accent; so, for *lóok at* vs. *look úp:*

He's not the person I was lóoking at.

He's not the person I was looking úp.

But some prepositions are weightier than others:

He's not the person I was looking áfter.

And a good deal more needs to be said both about the accent on prepositions in particular situations, and about the peculiar freedom of adpreps to be either accented or not (see Chapters 2 and 3).

As for separating adverbs (independent constituents) from adverb-particles (parts of phrasal verbs), it is proposed that a contrastive accent indicates the former. But this test will not serve by itself. Thus *give up, hold out,* and *throw away* are clearly phrasal verbs, yet we can have

We wanted you to hold óut, not give úp.

I wanted the stuff thrown awáy, not thrown back into the garage.

It is only in cases of ellipsis ("gapping") that the test works:

*I wanted the stuff thrown awáy, not back into the garage.

But then it works too well:

*I told him to move asíde, not awáy.

It would seem, if the notion of purely independent adverbs were valid, that *aside* and *away* in these two combinations should qualify; yet the test makes them appear to be adverb-particles. When we compare the example with

I told him to move úp, not dówn.

*I wanted you to pull it inside óut, not apárt.

I wanted you to pull it inside óut, not outside ín.

we find, I think, that the combined ellipsis and contrastive-accent test is effective only with what Fairclough (pp. 74–75) terms polarity, that is, with pairs like *off-on, up-down, in-out, fore-aft,* and the like; a pair like

The light went out. *The light went in.

indicates that *to go out* and *to go in* are not the same kind of combination.[9]

8. If the combination is transitive, the particle can *precede* a simple definite noun phrase (a proper name or *the* plus a common noun) without taking it as its object. This is a refinement of Test 4, the second half of which ("the particle can *follow* the noun object") is of little or no use anyway, since almost any adverb can follow:

*I saw yesterday John.

I saw John yesterday.

*He did neatly the work.

He did the work neatly.

*I left there the keys.

I left the keys there.

It is the ability to stand, as a unit, in the position which is otherwise privative to a unit verb, that counts:

I'm afraid to take on John in this contest.

You left out the caption.

Did you bring along the Joneses?

Some examples of more or less synonymous expressions:

Why don't you bring over John?

*Why don't you bring here John?

---

9. Another difficulty with the contrastive-accent test is that the slightest incongruity between the contrasted pairs can upset it. An extreme example is the possible mismatch between verb and particle. Something can curve either in or out, but can cave only in; something can bob up or down but can bow only down:

Did it curve in or out?

* Did it cave in or out?

Did it bob up or down?

* Did he bow up or down?

They dragged past the trailer.
*They dragged nearby the trailer.
They pushed in the door.
*They pushed inward the door.
They cut apart the orange.
*They cut in two the orange.
He scattered abroad the generations.
*He scattered afar the generations.
He finished up the report.
*He finished completely the report.

The same order can be maintained, of course, if the particle takes the noun as its own object; hence the need to distinguish between particles proper and pure prepositions:

She told on her friend.

That brought on the argument.

Some of the tests already mentioned help make the distinction, for example, Test 5:

She told on him. *She told him on.

That brought it on. *That brought on it.

I regard this test as the most dependable and will make the fullest use of it. The chief advantage is that it is not just an either-or test but can be varied by increasing or decreasing the semantic weight of the direct object, to reveal degrees of tightness of stereotyping. It fails to distinguish between literal and figurative uses of the particles,

He brought home the groceries.

He brought home the point in a convincing manner.

but I follow Fairclough in regarding all such cases as phrasal verbs anyway, with the distinction between literal and figurative viewed as secondary. The literal uses lie at the core, and figurative ones surround them at varying distances. The justification of Test 8 necessarily follows the discussion of the prosody of phrasal verbs (see Chapter 5).

9. Phrasal verbs can be defined by simply listing them. So far as I know, it has never been suggested that such a list might be exhaustive. For one thing, it is continually being added to. A new verb such as *to orbit* can immediately produce *to orbit out, to orbit away, to orbit around* (*The astronauts had been orbiting around for so long that they were as familiar with the moon's features as the earth's*). Compare *They* (the astronauts) *will then be helicoptered aboard the recovery carrier*.[10] For another, it would vary according to dialect. I could not, for example, include, for my dialect, the following which L. A. Hill offers as models of British usage:

He fell down and tore his trousers badly about. (p. 2)

We have a comedian here who takes the Prime Minister off wonderfully. (p. 111)

Choose out the biggest oranges for your mother. (p. 136)

When we were writing the invitations to our party, we missed Uncle Tom out by mistake. (p. 137)

Do you think the petrol will last out until we get home? (p. 137; "hold out" is acceptable.)

Jones opened out and passed the two men in front. (p. 141)

They became very poor, so they sold up their big house and went to live in a cheap hotel. (p. 191)

It has been suggested, however, that it might be feasible to list the particles. Mitchell says (p. 105), "Although it should be possible to establish a closed system of particles, this would hardly be practicable for the verbal component." Though the particle class is unquestionably far smaller than the verb class, deciding exactly what words it contains is harder than one might imagine. Meyer lists the following as the seventeen most productive (with frequencies in his corpus for the three most

10. *Life Atlantic*, 21 July 1969, p. 64, col. 1.

and the two least productive): *about, across, along, around,*[11]
aside (347), *away, back, by* (388), *down, in, off, on, out*
(871), *over* (735), *through, under, up* (1022). From L. A.
Hill's examples can be added *ahead, alongside, forth, forward,
past,* and *together,* and from Spasov's (pp. 13, 24) *aback,
above, after, again* (archaic), *apart, astray, asunder, athwart,
before, behind, below, between,* and *round.* Though not of
high frequency in the general language, a surprisingly large
number—perhaps as much as a fourth of the total—are nautical, or more common in nautical usage than elsewhere; besides
alongside and *athwart* these include *abaft, abeam, aboard, aft,
aloft, amidships, aport, ashore, astarboard, astern,* and *overboard.* For example,

They threw overboard the ballast.

He hauled aloft the pennon.

They set athwart the billets, for balance.

This contribution is understandable when one considers that
in no other occupation are directions and resultant positions
of such unremitting concern. To these we should probably
add *aground, askew, astride, atop, home, underground,*[12] and
underneath, for example,

It knocked aground the kite.

He pulled askew the covers.

They hauled underground the coal carts.

There are some uncertainties in the items already cited and
others that could be named,[13]—*aloud* and *to,* for example—es-

11. For British English it would be necessary to add *round* as a separate
item, if we follow L. A. Hill. The two, he says (p. 156), are interchangeable
only in the sense of "in all directions from a center," e.g. *look around,
go around, stand around, be* (*hang*) *around,* but not in *turn round* (circular
motion), *go round* ("make a circuit"), and so on.

12. Fairclough includes *go underground* among his phrasal verbs.

13. There are also some marginal candidates for inclusion. Fairclough
lists *pass beyond* and *penetrate beyond,* but I am unable to invent a satisfac-

pecially those which occur in only a few combinations:

He read aloud the story.[14]

*He spoke aloud the word.

He led astray his friend.

*He conducted (tempted, took) astray his friend.

I left behind the keys.[15]

*I threw (held, knocked) behind the stick.

They were carrying below the prisoners.

*They marched below the prisoners.

To has a number of firmly stereotyped uses,

We laid the feast before them and they fell to.

She was unconscious for a moment but then came to.

I pushed the door to.

The door went to.

Before dawn every morning, we had to stand to, ready for an enemy attack . . . , and then it was quite light we stood down again.[16]

. . . our culinary priest drew to the slides of his temple . . . [17]

But we are not as free to coin *The door banged* (*whanged, clapped, crashed,* etc.) *to* as to make the same combinations with *shut*. And some transitive uses are doubtful by Test 8:

She fainted, but a whiff of smelling salts brought her to.

*They brought to the victims.

---

tory example that will pass the definite-noun-phrase test. *This fuel will take you to the Great Barrier, but more is needed to propel the spaceship beyond* is no more satisfactory with *beyond* moved before the object noun phrase than *propel farther* would be in that same position.

14. Cf. Fairclough's example, p. 84, *the conscientious reader-aloud of bedtime stories.*

15. See p. 85.

16. L. A. Hill, p. 58.

17. Herman Melville, *Omoo,* chap. 16.

They brought the ship around and hove her to.

?They hove to the ship.

The problem here may be a sort of conflict of homonyms—*to bring to the victims* is too reminiscent of *to bring something to someone*—the pure prepositional use of *to*. But uncertainties also attend other combinations, whether limited in range or not. Should we include, for example, particles which themselves consist of more than one word? There are a few which are closely allied, semantically, to one-word particles, and qualify by Test 8:

They brought aboard the passengers.

They brought on board the passengers.

They took ashore the passengers.

*They took on shore the passengers.

It brings out the facts.

It brings to light the facts.

*It brings to view the facts.

Furthermore, a small number of adjectives and infinitives behave like particles and will be related to them in the treatment to follow (see Chapter 6):

He cut open the melon and cut out the seeds.

*She cut small the paper dolls.

He let go the reins and let off the harness.

*The turnkey let eat the prisoners.

Finally, increasing the information value (or the length—these two factors are concomitant) of the object noun phrase gradually increases the possibilities:

They took on shore a passenger or two.

*They took gladly (immediately) a passenger or two.

They took gladly (immediately) whatever passengers were willing to go.

It appears that while the class of particles is restricted, it is not closed by any standard that will not do violence to natural language.

The core particles are adverbial, and may or may not be prepositional as well. They are not pure prepositions, as can be appreciated by comparing synonyms. In the following, the star marks examples which would be unacceptable without a prepositional object—sign of a pure preposition:

*She looked disgustedly at the dirty platform and walked from (the platform).

She looked disgustedly at the dirty platform and walked off (the platform).

*He met his friend and walked beside (his friend).

He met his friend and walked alongside (his friend).

*We came to the arch and walked beneath (the arch).

We came to the arch and walked underneath (the arch).

A very few instances can be found where pure prepositions occur in combinations without an object. There are the dialectal *come* (*go*) *with* and the standard *do* (or *go*) *without:*

Wait a minute and I'll come with.

If there isn't enough to buy what we need we'll simply have do without.

Other instances of unresolved prepositions are those against which Fairclough warned (p. 113) that "It is necessary . . . to distinguish between the regular process of contraction [for example, *to sail ahead of the passenger boat* shortened to *to sail ahead*] . . . and the context-determined ellipsis of the complement . . . *instead of getting sixty nations voting against it we got . . . fifty nations voting for it, . . . instead of getting sixty nations voting against we got fifty nations voting for.*" The status of particles as prepositions will be discussed in Chapter 2.

Another possible candidate for listing would be the set of

verbs that never, or seldom, occur without a particle. I have not collected these, but can exemplify with *to stride:*

How did he get there? *He strode.

How did he get there? He walked.

What did he do? He strode (walked) off.

(We note that this verb is partially defective. *Stridden* would not be heard nowadays, and even the present-tense forms *stride* and *strides* are infrequent.) Other examples are *to shore up* and *to sum up.*

CHAPTER 2

Adpreps and Dual Functions

Adverbs and prepositions. Particles that form the most typical phrasal verbs are the ones that function now as adverbs, now as prepositions. One can frequently add a prepositional function by simply repeating a noun already in the context:

He came to the end of the bridge and jumped off (the bridge).

He came to the water and jumped in (the water).

He came to the table and crawled under (the table).

He caught up with the parade and walked behind (the parade).

With *off* and *on,* a reflexive pronoun often makes the conversion:

He put the coat on (himself).

She pulled off (herself, her finger) the ring.

More often, the unmentioned context supplies the missing prepositional object:

She pulled the tablecloth off (the table).

He pulled the door to (the jamb).

Throw in (the deal) a larger bonus.

Throw in (the pot) your money.

The movie was so popular they held it over (the time limit).

She looked at us disgustedly and walked off (the scene).

She finally came to (her senses).

Prepositional objects may be more or less explicit, more or less covert:

He came to the road and struggled across (the road).

He came to the road and struggled along (his way) *or* on (his way).

The crew went below (decks).

The extent to which an underlying preposition is present to our minds of course varies. In

> They set up the target.
>
> He threw down a challenge.

we seem to have particles with no prepositional counterpart at all:[1] *up* = *upright*, *down* = *downward* in a figurative sense. With the particles *off*, *down*, *out*, *over*, and *through* and possibly some others, there is an apparent reversal of the underlying object if the particle is taken as a preposition. Thus in

> She brushed off the suit.
>
> I wiped out the sink.
>
> She papered over the door and window by mistake.
>
> We flushed down the floor of the garage.

it seems as if the meaning should be "She brushed the lint off the suit," "I wiped the dirt out of the sink," "She put the paper over the door," etc. These can be contrasted with

> She brushed off the lint.
>
> I wiped out the dirt.

in which the direct object is explicit and the prepositional object is suppressed. But a better analysis, it seems to me, is in terms of there being no prepositional object at all in a sentence like *She brushed off the clothes* (if there were, we would expect *She brushed off them*, not *She brushed them off*), but rather an initial adverbialization that creates the phrasal verb *to brush off*, and then an extension of meaning (or a shift in the case relationships) that parallels exactly what happens with simple verbs like *provide, present, sterilize*, etc.:

> We provided the goods. We provided the people with the goods.
>
> They presented the prize. They presented the winner with the prize.

1. One may be confected, however: *He set up (the vertical dimension) the target.*

They sterilized the germs. They sterilized the instruments
of their germs.

(The exchange between the object and the thing or person
affected works both ways, as witness

I believe the man. I believe the man's word.)

What we get, then, is an initial stereotyping into a phrasal
verb, and then a reciprocation of the case relationships, so
that in

Flush out the dirt.

Flush out the mains.

there is no longer any preposition to account for. The same
reciprocation occurs with phrasal verbs in which there was
no explicit preposition plus object to begin with:

Clean up the mess.

Clean up the room.

Stake out the plainclothesmen.

Stake out the suspects.[2]

---

2. *Through* is curiously restricted. When it precedes a concrete noun
and the noun is not further modified, it is taken in a prepositional relationship to the noun:

* She always soaks through the clothes before scrubbing them.

She always soaks the clothes through before scrubbing them.

The water soaked through the clothes.

The water soaked the clothes through.

* He ran through the man with the rapier.

He ran the man through with the rapier.

The rapier ran through the man.

The rapier ran the man through.

They put (hammered, drove) through the legislation. (abstract noun)

She always soaks through whatever clothes need washing before putting
them in the machine. (further modification)

There is no such restriction, for example, with *off*:

We flushed off the floor before scrubbing it.

We flushed the floor off before scrubbing it.

The water flushed off the floor.

The water flushed the floor off.

The next-to-last example may be taken in either sense. (The last one
is irrelevantly ambiguous.)

For the particles that oscillate between preposition and adverb I use the term *prepositional adverb*.[3] In addition to these there are some particles that are uniquely adverbs, a number in particular using the prefix *a-*:

He ran away. (*He ran away school.)
I walked home. (*I walked home my apartment.)
They ran ashore.
She turned aside.

(Both sets qualify as particles by the definite-noun-phrase test, explained as item 8 in Chapter 1 and covered fully in Chapter 5. So, for adverbs,

She turned aside the criticism. She turned the criticism aside.
They pushed ashore the dory. They pushed the dory ashore.
We drove home the point. We drove the point home.

And for prepositional adverbs:

She knocked down the argument. She knocked the argument down.
They pushed in the dory. They pushed the dory in.

The fact that not all *a-* prefixed adverbs are phrasal-verb particles, that is, that

He set the house afire. ?He set afire the house.
She set her arms akimbo. *She set akimbo her arms.

do not qualify, will be dealt with as part of the question of the semantic features of the particles.)

Adpreps versus adverbs and prepositions. The variable status of the prepositional adverb can be illustrated by triply ambiguous sentences like

He ran down the road.
She swept off the stage.
We backed up the stream.

3. "Adverbial preposition" would serve just as well except that it is the adverbial rather than the prepositional use that is more relevant to this study.

If the particle is taken as an adverb, the corresponding pronominalizations will be

He ran it down. (disparaged it)

She swept it off. (cleaned it)

We backed it up. (clogged it)

If it is taken as a preposition, the pronominalizations and meanings will be

He ran down it. (did his running somewhere down the
road)

She swept off it. (did her sweeping somewhere not on the
stage)

We backed up it. (did our backing at some point upstream)

Because these are purely prepositional, they do not interest
us—*back up,* for example, is not a constituent, and therefore
is not a phrasal verb; in transformational terms, the preposition
is "outside" the verb phrase and has a purely locative meaning.[4]
But there is a third possibility, with the same pronominalizations as in the last set but with a different meaning:

He ran down it. (descended it)

She swept off it. (departed from it majestically)

We backed up it. (ascended it in reverse direction)

The position of the pronoun (almost but not quite obligatory,
as will be seen later) argues that the particle is a preposition.
But the contrast between the last set and the preceding one
reveals that now the particle is a constituent of the phrases
run down, sweep off, and *back up.* In other words, *down, off,*
and *up* belong as much to the phrasal verb as they do
to the prepositional phrase. It is a case of dual constituency.

4. See Charles J. Fillmore, "The Case for Case," in Emmon Bach and
Robert T. Harms, *Universals in Linguistic Theory* (New York, Holt, Rine-
hart, and Winston, 1968), p. 12.

For particles in this double function I adopt A. A. Hill's term *adprep*.[5]

While pronominalization and position show quite graphically the difference between the particle as adverb and the particle as adprep, for example,

He ran the flag up. He ran up the flag. He ran it up. *He ran up it.

He climbed up the pole. *He climbed the pole up.[6] He climbed up it. *He climbed it up.

the difference between the particle as adprep and the particle as pure preposition does not yield to this test. But it reveals itself in at least two other ways. The first is in the possibilities of insertion. With adpreps there are two such, corresponding to the two affinities. The first affinity is with the verb proper—the connection with the verb is protected and the particle is split off from the prepositional object:

He ran up, pell-mell, the first hill he saw.

The second affinity is with the prepositional object—the particle is now joined to the latter and split off from the verb:

He ran, pell-mell, up the first hill he saw.

Both these are normal, as against what happens with a pure

5. I redefine the term slightly. For Hill (I am inferring from Taha, who borrows it) it represents the class of particles whose members can be either adverb or preposition, now one, now the other. This is the sense in which I use the term *prepositional adverb*. As redefined, *adprep* is taken in its functional sense: it is a prepositional adverb which is an adverb and a preposition at one and the same time. It is, as will be shown, a collapsed compound preposition.

Though I have not seen the unpublished study by Ranko Bugarski, my impression is that it embodies the same concept of dual affinity: *He looked over his shoulder,* for example, is "a colligational blend of phrasal verb and prep-phrase, with *over* collocationally attracted both to the left and to the right" (personal letter, 10 September 1969).

6. This is acceptable as "He climbed the pole upward (rather than downward)," that is, in a contrastive context. But *climb* is then a simple verb, not phrasal: *He climbed it.—Which way?—Up.*

preposition like *toward:*
 *He ran toward, pell-mell, the first hill he saw.
 He ran, pell-mell, toward the first hill he saw.
Compare also
 He either crawled up, or was carried up, the stairs.
 ?He either crawled from, or was carried from, the house.
And, with *along,*
 They sat along the paths in the park.
 They sat drowsily along the paths in the park.
 *They sat along drowsily the paths in the park.
 They strolled along the paths in the park.
 They strolled drowsily along the paths in the park.
 They strolled along drowsily the paths in the park.
in which *strolled along* can be a constituent but *sat along* cannot. If a correlative adverb such as *first* (in *first . . . then*) or *now* (as in *now . . . now*) can, though with difficulty, be inserted between a pure preposition and its object, that position may be *preferred* with the adprep:
 He talks first in one language and then another.
 ?He talks in first one language and then another.
 ?He runs first down one hill and then another.
 He runs down first one hill and then another.[7]
 Historically, the possible disjuncture *after* the particle is a

7. Jespersen both sees and fails to see this contrast. In III 13.9₁₃ he uses the criterion of the intervening element to distinguish the adverb from the preposition, to prove that *over* in *Thinking over again the reply I made* is an adverb. But he then (13.9₂) distinguishes an adverb in *I'll see him through* from a preposition in *We saw through the secret,* apparently without realizing that a sentence like *We saw through, definitely (clearly,* etc.), *every stratagem he tried* is acceptable, which by his criterion proves *through* to be an adverb. Though he later (13.9₄) cites examples exactly like this (*I came across, at the very bottom, the manuscript of the preceding narrative*), he only says that the object here is "rather of the whole combination than of the preposition" and does not recognize a special subtype of phrasal verb.

residue of the old division:

He ran up / the hill = He upran the hill, he ascended the hill.[8]

The second bit of evidence for a prep-adprep contrast is phonological. It can be cited in more than one way, but the easiest to hear is where the particle is maneuvered to final position in a relative clause. Referring to an athlete who has run a race in a gymnasium, we might say, using a pure preposition,

Show me the gym he rán in.

Referring to a roundup, we might say, using an adverb particle,

Show me the cattle he rán ín.

But referring to a fugitive who takes refuge in a house, we use an adprep and have a choice:

Show me the house he rán in.

Show me the house he ran ín.

---

8. See Tauno F. Mustanoja, *A Middle English Syntax* (Helsinki, Société Néophilologique, 1960) p. 346. I suspect that this is also reflected in a curious restriction on *in* and *into*. Both can be used of material objects:

He broke in (into) our house.

They jumped in (into) the water.

But only *into* seems to be admissible with abstractions:

He broke into our meeting.

He cut into our conversation.

He walked into our conclave.

It is as if *break in* were still felt as *in-break,* meaning "to enter." *Enter* is inappropriate with the last three examples. Compare also

They entered the room.

They entered into an agreement.

For the most part, the positioning of the particle before the verb has been completely specialized—*to offset* is felt as a single verb consisting of prefix plus base—and what may have offered itself at one time as a choice to the speaker, to be made in accordance with the prosody of the sentence, is no longer so. Our reaction to the following today shows the semantic divergence: "He for his own part would have been delighted to pardon the harmless little boyish frolic, had not its unhappy publicity rendered it impossible to *look the freak over*" (W. M. Thackeray, *Pendennis* [New Century Library, Thomas Nelson and Son, n.d.; first published 1850], p. 222). The prosodic choices that will be discussed in Chapter 4 are similarly being narrowed by the stereotyping of the remaining positions of the particle (see Chapter 10) but this process still has a long way to go.

Adpreps and compound prepositions. Adpreps are portmanteau words, fusions of elements that are syntactically distinct but semantically identical. Syntactically they resemble compound prepositions, in which both the syntactic and the semantic features are kept relatively more distinct. The following are syntactically comparable:

He walked across the road.
He walked across across the road.
He walked over across the road.
They penetrated beyond the barrier.
They penetrated beyond beyond the barrier.
They penetrated through beyond the barrier.

The separation in fact occurs when an object noun is inserted, though the second element undergoes a stylistic change:

*They pushed *over* the pram *over* the road.
They pushed *over* the pram *across* the road.
*He drove *off* the chickens *off* the lawn.
He drove *off* the chickens *from* the lawn.
*He ran *up* the flag *up* the pole.
He ran *up* the flag *on* the pole.
*They pulled *aboard* the sailors *aboard* the liner.
They pulled *aboard* the sailors *onto* the liner.

The resemblance of the adprep to a compound preposition is seen in the regular fused forms which likewise are changed when separated, as against the unfused forms which do not change:

He let the air *out of* my tires.
*He let *out* the air *of* my tires.
He let *out* the air *from* my tires.
She pulled the carriage *into* the house.
*She pulled *in* the carriage *to* the house.
She pulled *in* the carriage *inside* the house.
He held the money *back from* his clients.
He held *back* the money *from* his clients.

I can't get the idea *through to* those people.

I can't get *through* the idea *to* those people.

Over across, up through, down along, back from, etc. illustrate the freedom we have to create compound prepositions. But the fused ones—in which the spelling sometimes shows the tighter link—are the ones that most resemble adpreps. With adpreps we have complete overlap; with a word such as *into* we have fusion; with *over across* we have addition:

He walked in—in the house → He walked in the house. (overlap)

He walked in—to the house → He walked into the house. (fusion)

He jumped out—out the window → He jumped out the window. (overlap)

He jumped out—of the window → He jumped out of the window. (fusion)

It was drawn near—near the other side → It was drawn near the other side. (overlap)

It was drawn near—to the other side → It was drawn near to the other side. (fusion)

He jumped off—off the step → He jumped off the step. (overlap)

He jumped off—of the step → He jumped off of the step. (fusion)

He ran down—down the road → He ran down the road. (overlap)

He ran down along the road. (no change, addition)

Hold on!—What on?—On the railing! (*on* actually split, *on on*)

Hold on!—What to?—To the railing! (addition)

The semantic redundancy in a sentence like *He jumped over over the fence* is probably what accounts for their unacceptability, but it parallels that of examples where the verb already incorporates a feature that the particle repeats. Thus *pass = go by* and *penetrate = go through,* yet we can say

He passed (went by) by the house.

It penetrated (went through) through the cloth.

Fusions to right and left. We find both leftward fusions and rightward fusions of the particle. The rightward fusions produce the lexically consecrated compound prepositions like *into, onto, out of, alongside of, inside of,* and the like. They tend, but not completely, to revert to the condition of pure preposition:

You're going-along with your sister. ("accompanying her," leftward fusion)

You're going, along-with your sister. ("besides," rightward fusion)[9]

As more or less pure preposition, its first element may then conceivably, though not normally, be repeated adverbially to the left:

He jumped *out*—out of the window. He jumped out from the window.

Or—and this is the same thing—a redundant, and synonymous, particle may be added; in the following, *stick up* and *stick out* would mean the same:

Wrecks stuck up out of the water everywhere.[10]

With a comma break, repetition becomes acceptable. The following illustrate this and also illustrate the rightward and leftward fusions:

It has dwindled down, to the point that there is practically nothing left.

It has dwindled, down to the point that . . .

9. See Fairclough, p. 76: *She dropped her hand and moved away from him* shows by polarity with *towards* that *"away from* is in the same relationship to *away* as *out of* to *out."*

10. Example from L. A. Hill, p. 145.

It has dwindled down, down to the point that . . .
*It has declined down, down to the point that . . .
It has declined, down to the point that . . .
*It has declined down, down to the point that . . .

Here *dwindle down,* in spite of its apparent redundancy, makes an acceptable phrasal verb, while *decline down* does not; but *down to* makes an acceptable compound preposition in any case. The verbs *to reduce* and *to diminish* behave similarly: *reduce* is like *dwindle* (*It reduces down quite satisfactorily*); *diminish* is like *decline* (*It diminishes down quite satisfactorily*). (We notice that etymology is irrelevant: both *reduce* and *diminish* are Latinate forms from Middle English.) Other examples:

They've gone off, to the races.
They've gone, off to the races.
They've gone off, off to the races.
He was running away, from danger.
He was running, away from danger.
He was running away, away from danger.
He hurried back, from the hotel.
He hurried, back from the hotel.
He hurried back, back from the hotel.

When a rightward fusion produces a new preposition, it will of course have its own meaning:

He walked out (*not* out of) the door.
He walked out of (*not* out) the house.

Inseparability is further evidence of fusion:

They pushed the piston out of (out from) the cylinder.
They pushed out the piston from the cylinder.
*They pushed out the piston of the cylinder.
He cheated me out of my money.
*He cheated me out.

As might be expected, the dual attachment of the particle

makes it possible to iterate it:

He walked round and round the square.

They went over and over the figures.

and to combine it:

Run up over the hill.

They called to him from the other side of the hill and he
ran up over.

Come back up over the wall.

He was going to climb up through the trees, but I don't
know whether he's up through them yet or not.

Run out in the yard and play.[11]

There are leftward fusions in which the particle becomes
as firmly attached to the verb as, with rightward ones, it is
attached to another particle. Those which concern us here—involving adpreps—result in combinations of verbs with the
prepositional function of the particle, a type which has been
excluded from this study. (Other fusions of verb and particle
will be treated in Chapter 9, "Stereotyping".) To illustrate
with contrasting pairs, unfused and fused:

He walked across the road = He walked across across the
road.

He came across the missing papers = *He came across across
the missing papers.

He ran over the bridge = He ran over over the bridge.

He ran over the child = *He ran over over the child.

I could see through the tunnel = I could see through
through the tunnel.

11. These can be interpreted variously, depending on whether the prepositional or the adverbial function is paramount. Thus "Run-up over the
hill" is a possible reading, with *over* carrying the prepositional function,
or "Run up-over the hill," where both *over* and *up* are prepositional and
up takes the space represented by *over* as its object. This is common
in slightly substandard expressions like *The puppy crawled in under the
table.* There are certain restrictions on the order of these combinations,
which are discussed on pp. 132–134.

*I could see through through his deceit.

He came by the house = He came by by the house.

*He came by by a fortune.[12]

The verb-particle fusion can be tested with constructions which force an unacceptable separation of the two (Fairclough, p. 15):

*The missing papers across which he came.

*Over which child did he run?

*The deceit through which I could see.

*The fortune by which he came.

As Spasov points out (pp. 43–44), there is almost unlimited variety in the degrees of fusion to left and to right.

---

12. Gradience is rampant between figurative and nonfigurative, because any nonfigurative use today can become a new figure tomorrow while still retaining some of its nonfigurative characteristics. If we compare *to look through* and *to glance through,* both meaning "to examine," we find that the first seems to be a figure of longer standing, in view of the ease of the literal *He picked up the glass and looked through* and the difficulty of the figurative ?*He picked up the papers and looked through*—the latter strikes us as like *He picked up the papers and examined.* But

He went to the window and glanced through.

He picked up the book and glanced through.

seem normal.

CHAPTER 3

Adpreps and Adverbs: Order and Accent

Mobility of the particle. The most obvious syntactic difference between the adverbial particle in *He ran up the flag* (derived, to be sure, from an adprep: *He ran up the pole the flag*) and the adprep in *He climbed up the tree* is the mobility of the two particles:

He ran up the flag. He ran the flag up.

He climbed up the tree. *He climbed the tree up.

Yet this restriction is not absolute. A few of the adprep particles retain in Modern English their old freedom with transitive verbs to go either before the object or after it in what appear to be identical functions.[1] Kennedy speaks (p. 17) of a "postpositive preposition" and Poutsma[2] of a "displaced preposition." Examples:

You can travel the wórld óver (all over the world) and not find anything nicer.

---

1. See George O. Curme, *Syntax* (New York, D. C. Heath and Co., 1931), p. 569. There was also the freedom—now fossilized and semantically stereotyped—to put the particle before the verb: *to overlook, to upset, to backfire* (where we do get a new term by this process it is semantically specialized: *to backfire* does not mean the same as *to fire back*). In a strange reversal of habit, the thing that speakers of English once did with great freedom is the very thing they most strongly avoid now, though with other complements it is possible:

He talks fast, his fast talking.

He talks on, *his on talking.

They buy eagerly, their eager buying.

They buy up, *their up buying.

He broke the record, his record breaking.

He broke down, *his down breaking.

2. Poutsma, Part II (Groningen, P. Noordhoff, 1926), sec. II, p. 89.

I'm not sure that I can live the dáy thróugh (through the day).

He glanced the order through[3] (through the order).

He works the clóck aróund (around the clock).

I pass these idle arguments by (by these idle arguments).

I wonder if you'll look over it[4] (look it over).

That these are fossils is evident in their restrictions. First, dialectal; the following are not standard:

In stooping her over to kiss her.[5]

They ran him over = They ran over him.[6]

Second, semantic restrictions; we sense a difference in transitivity nowadays between the following pairs:

We pondered over it a long time.

We pondered it over a long time.

She got over the disagreeable interview.

She got the disagreeable interview over.

He saw through that business.

He saw that business through (its difficulties).

Third, restriction to certain idioms or certain verbs:

She is . . . at the beck and call of the employer the day through[7] (the day through = all day).

Will you look (glance, go, run) over it with me? *and* Will you look (glance, run) it over with me? *but* *Will you go it over with me?

3. Nevil Shute, *On the Beach* (New York, Wm. Morrow, 1957), p. 145.

4. Graduate student, University of Colorado, 18 May 1961, referring to a thesis outline.

5. Poutsma, Part II (Groningen, 1926) sec. II, p. 89.

6. Figuratively, *He had no sooner run it hastily over* [a letter], *than he exclaimed* . . . ," Sir Walter Scott, *Rob Roy* (London, Everyman Edition, 1906; reprinted 1963), p. 76. This would still be heard, I think, especially if the context permitted the *over* to suggest repetition. One musician might say to another, *Let's run this over again.*

7. Kruisinga, sec. 1418.

As a rule, the same mobility that distinguishes adverbial particles from adpreps when there are object nouns present, settles into an outright opposition with personal pronouns:

The marble rolled over the carpet → The marble rolled over it. *The marble rolled it over.

The cleaners rolled over the carpet (rolled the carpet over) → The cleaners rolled it over. *The cleaners rolled over it.

This restriction is the one most often cited when the difference between adverb and adprep is mentioned.[8] Yet it is no more absolute than the other, and in this case the freedom is productive, not merely embalmed in a few relics:

The lady bade her take away the fool; therefore, I say again, take her away.—Sir, I bade them take away you.

If you want to ease your mind by blowing up somebody, come out into the court and blow up me.[9]

I knew that the school board contemplated throwing out Spanish in order to throw out me.[10]

We'll run down [summarize] thém for you.[11]

He's just lucky I ain't sewin' up hím![12]

Fancy taking on hér![13]

. . . you may give up society without any great pang . . . ,

8. "In the active voice a pronoun object must come between the verb and adverbial," Alan Healey, "English Idioms," *Kivung* 1:80 (1968); "It is unlikely that a personal pronoun would ever stand after the particle," Fairclough, p. 62.

9. This example and the preceding one are quoted from Shakespeare and Dickens by Poutsma, pp. 423–424.

10. Personal communication.

11. Radio announcer, Station KNX, Los Angeles.

12. Spoken by Wishbone on "Rawhide" television program, 11 March 1960, referring to someone who got his clothes torn and might have torn himself as well.

13. Said by a World Affairs Week Conference (University of Colorado, 11 April 1961) speaker, who was British, referring to a little old lady who had been caught unawares by a newsreel photographer at a hearing of the House Committee on Un-American Activities—he was suggesting the consequences of her being called as a hostile witness.

but severe are the mortifications and pains you have if
society gives up you.[14]
They will cut up [lampoon] mé sometimes.[15]
The following invented examples seem acceptable to me:
Leave out hím if you don't have enough for everybody.
As between the man and the company, I figured that if
I was going to buy out hím I might as well buy out ít.
And this invented example seems to me to be impossible to
reverse without changing the meaning:
His plan all along was not to eulogize mè but to run down
hér.[16]
Cases of conjunction clearly allow end position of the pronoun:
The present Executive Secretary declines to take responsibil-
ity for arranging another meeting in which a minority
can panic the authorities and by so doing tie up him and
the MLA administrative staff . . . in negotiations . . . [17]
Bring along him and her.
His scheme was to show up you or me as a liar.
The idea was to play off you against your sister.
And so do reflexive pronouns:
Who shall I bring along? Jack and Alice?—Just bring along
yourself, and we'll do fine.
On this list, Mr. Agnew, am I supposed to check off mysélf?
Or you?—Just check off mé—leave your name for the
present.
The possibility of end position for other pronouns has never

14. *Pendennis*, p. 715, n. 8.
15. Harvard University teaching fellow, 27 November 1968, referring
to students in his class.
16. It is possible of course to say *to rún hér dówn,* with three successive
accents. But this shifts the balance of contrast: instead of primary contrast
on *me* and *her* and secondary on the verbs, the contrast on the verbs is
raised to equal status.
17. *PMLA* 84:346 (1969).

been denied, though it has been called unlikely. One example, spoken by the operator of a Xerox machine:

The lights won't pick up thís.

The argument that pronouns cannot come at the end puts the cart before the horse. What needs to be asked is what it is that end position confers, and what it is about personal pronouns that makes them substantially less likely than nouns to have that something conferred on them. It is obvious from the examples that the pronouns are all contrastive. The significance of this will be discussed along with the larger question of the prosody of phrasal verbs.

The test of accent. Next to order, accent has been most often used to illustrate the difference between adverbs, adpreps, and prepositions.[18] Live proposes (p. 439) as her test frame for adverb ("Group 1") in contrast to preposition ("Group 3") the passive voice with the particle in final position:

It (the button) was sewed ón.

It (the dress) was séwed on.

—and the same test can be applied to relative clauses:

This is the report he passed ón (forwarded, *adverb*).

This is the report he pássed on (approved, *preposition*).

(A shift of accent here would be contrastive.) We have already noted (Chapter 2) the three-way contrast in

---

18. Taha uses it (pp. 117–118) to distinguish between the prepositional and adverbial uses of the particles. Palmer feels (p. 182) that the adverb and the preposition are consistently distinguished by accent. He cites

The plane that the passenger fléw in.

The plane that the pilot flew ín.

But Daniel Jones cites (*An Outline of English Phonetics*, 8th ed. [New York, E. P. Dutton and Co., Inc., 1956], sec. 992) examples of unaccented adverbs:

He let the fíre out.

Before you go out, better put your cóat on.

And a little change in the information content of Palmer's example reverses the accents: *What's your bróther doing?—He's flying his pláne in.*

Show me the gym he rán in (*preposition*).
Show me the cattle he rán ín (*adverb*).
Show me the house he rán in (ran ín) (*adprep*).
where the in-between status of the adprep shows up in the possibility of accenting either way. The same happens in Live's test frame:

Is that the spot that was passed bý (pássed by)?
Is that the bridge that was crossed óver (cróssed over)?

And when we spell out the duality by repeating the adprep, or by using two particles one of which is the adverb part and the other the preposition part, the first gets the accent, the second not (the first two examples are hypothetical):

Is that the bridge that was crossed óver over?
Is that the pole that was climbed úp up?
Is that the house that was run ínto? (*adv.* + *prep.*).
Is that the house that was rún into? (into *treated as unit prep.*)[19]
Is that the window that was jumped oút of?
Is that the window that was júmped out of? (*out of* treated as unit preposition = *from*).

But even here, fluctuations in the information content and other variables may invalidate the test. We could probably dismiss an instance of multiple accents in emphatic utterance as an exception, the same as we would dismiss contrastive accent:

Boy, did hé gét sát ón!

___

19. The two uses of *into* contrast in
That's the car I bumped ínto. See the dent here on the side where I hit it with mine?
That's the car I búmped into. See the scratch here on my leg that I got when I hit it walking last night?
Only the first, with the adprep, has a passive: *That's the car that was bumped ínto* (*búmped into*). The second has no passive and allows *into* to be replaced by a pure preposition such as *on* or *against: That's the car I búmped against.*

(compare *ábsólútely, ábsólútelý*); and we could also dismiss those cases where after the nuclear accent everything else is de-accented, resulting sometimes in ambiguity:

> búttons been sewed on yet?

Have my

But there remain cases where by other criteria the particle has to be regarded as a preposition, and it nevertheless is or may be accented. This is more often true of the longer prepositions, but not necessarily of them only. The unacceptability of **Did you lean it against?* (by contrast with the acceptability of *Did you lean it out?*) shows *against* to be a preposition, not an adverb nor an adprep, and yet in

> Is that the wall it was léaned against (leaned agáinst)?

we have a choice, with no necessary suggestions of contrastive accent. Live's example *was góne òver* (p. 434) is not limited to that pattern, but may occur either way:

> The trouble is that his reports were never carefully góne over (gone óver).

(*Go over* is necessarily a preposition, since **He went them over*, unlike *He talked them over*, is unacceptable). The most we can say is that prepositions tend not to carry the accent, whether the verb is passive or not. There are synonyms and near-synonyms that may work in opposite ways, like *look áfter* (or *lóok after*) as against *wáit on:*

> Having that child as a guest is a nuisance. Her mother expects her to be looked áfter all the time, to be wáited on.
>
> What did you gó for, the milk?
> What did you go áfter (gó after), the milk?
> What were they spéaking of?
> What were they speaking abóut (spéaking about)?

The last example treats *about* like any other content word occupying the position of sentence accent and information

peak: we know they were speaking and now we inquire
  What was the speakers' súbject?
It would be most unnatural to weight *of* in this way to get
spéaking óf.[20]

20. The same vacillation is found with the fused verb-particle combinations, in which the particle was seen to behave like a preposition (pp.
35–36). With some, it is more usual to accent the verb; with others there
is a choice:
  It is something not easily cóme by.
  It's a pretext so easily séen through (seen thróugh).
  Which was the dog that was rún over (run óver)?

CHAPTER 4

The Prosody of Phrasal Verbs

Phrasal verbs by the simplest definition must contain a verb proper and something else. What that something else is can be disregarded while we ask whether there is any significance in the simple fact of there being more than one word.

There are three ways in which it could be important. One is how the prosody is affected. Given the fact that English is normally limited to one stress per word, and that the number of stresses determines the number of accents that can be put in a sentence, the more words there are the wider the speaker's choice will be in where the accents are to fall and how many there can be.[1] The second is arrangement. If in place of one word there are two, and they do not have to remain side by side and in the same order, whatever it is that order contributes to meaning will be enhanced. Third is what might be called a kind of semantic spreading out, an analytic tendency whereby instead of packing a fat bundle of semantic features into one word, matters can be made more flexible by packing thinner bundles into two or more words. The three intertwine, and I treat them together as prosody.

First, with respect to semantic spreading out versus semantic overloading, most speakers would probably not be happy with a sentence like

He discarded the trash and stowed the bags.

---

1. The question has been raised for German: *Hilfe bringen* distributes the sentence accents more advantageously than *helfen*. See K.-H. Daniels, *Substantivierungstendenzen in der deutschen Gegenwartssprache.* Sprache und Gemeinschaft: Studien, vol. III (Düsseldorf, Schwann, 1963). My information is from the review by Leslie Seiffert, *Journal of Linguistics* 4:101–102 (1968).

The semantic elements actually in contrast here are mixed in with others, and are not properly highlighted. This is corrected in

He threw óut the trash and packed ín the bags.

Similarly, whereas the next two sentences are normal enough,

Shall we sell it or discárd it?

Shall we sell it or throw it awáy?

nevertheless there is a semantic feature shared by both *sell* and *discard,* or both *sell* and *throw away,* namely the meaning "to dispose of," which is not factored out. All three verbs, *sell, discard,* and *throw away,* are the same in that feature but different in others. If the speaker wants to bring out the difference—to highlight *"getting* money by *selling"* and *"not* getting money by *discarding"*—the second sentence enables him to do so, simply by de-accenting the repeated element, which is *away,* the "disposing of" part:

Shall we séll it or thrów it away?

(If the feature is not repeated, its carrier will not be de-accented. Here *discard* is satisfactory, but *throw away* is no less so:

*Shall we keep it or thrów it away?

Shall we keep it or discard it [throw it awáy]?)

A similar spreading out—with accentual freedom—is essential for a phenomenon that can be termed "rectification accent." It is generally supposed that to get a yes-no emphasis on a verb, one must accent the auxiliary, and if there is no auxiliary, then a *do* must be supplied to carry the accent:

Why aren't you going?—I ám going.

Why didn't you make up the beds?—I díd make them up.

The supposed dependence on an auxiliary really amounts only to dependence on an element that is semantically barren, or relatively so. The auxiliary, as the carrier of tense and mode but not of lexical content, is ideal for the purpose, but there

are other ways of getting semantically low-content words and
the phrasal verb is one of them. This can be appreciated best
by examining an opposite case. If we say

How did he die?—They stárved him to death.
How did he die?—*They pút him to death.

the second is unacceptable because the relatively empty word
put supplies no information, and the intent of the answer is
to supply the information called for. But if we say

He deserved to die. Why didn't someone take care of
it?—They pút him to death!

laying the accent on *put* has the same effect as in

They díd kill him!

Though we generally think of sentences like these in connection
with affirming and denying, actually they are part of the more
general phenomenon of de-accenting elements that are repeated
or presupposed. In *I díd write it!—You dídn't write it!* the
nuclear accent is not shifted to the auxiliary merely to have
it there, but in part to get it off the repeated *write*. The accent
is required for the yes-no emphasis, but it would be misleading
if it fell on a content word:

I'm not sure about what tó review and what nót to review
(= I'm not sure what I shóuld review and what I
shóuldn't).
That's the sense in whích I meant it! (= That's the sense
in which I díd mean it.)

However we view it, pluri-word verbs still fulfill the role:

These two things don't always gó together.
Why didn't you throw it awáy?—I thréw it away. You just
weren't paying attention.

Compare the ineffectiveness of

These two things aren't always connécted.
Why didn't you discárd it?—I discárded it.

(The first could be effectively spread out by adding some

redundancy:

These two things are not always connécted with each other.)

Spreading out is also necessary if the speaker wants to in crease the number of accents. Consider a tourist who is bargain ing for a combination deal including both travel and accommo dations. He might say

If you thrów in the hotél, I'll take it.

Here *throw in* is no more affirmative than *add* would be. But if the agent has already half offered the hotel and there is a question of affirming the uncertain bonus, the speaker might say

If you thrów ín the hotél, it's a deal.

—which is more than can be said with *add*, unless an accent-carrier is supplied:

If you wíll ádd the hotél, it's a deal.

The difference in assertiveness between the examples

Yóu discárd that!

Yóu thrów thát awáy!

is clear. The phrasal verb not only adds an accent of its own, but by a rule which permits the speaker to accent a demonstra-tive that would be unaccented in final position, it enables him to add another on the word *that*.

The number of accent positions also works to advantage in the well-known emotional backshift of accent. This is famil-iar in cases like

The héll you say.

I just háte it that she's so careless with money.

Applied to phrasal verbs it gives examples like

Avocados? Lord, we've had all we could eat plus dozens to gíve away.

2. Without redundancy, one can still have a rectification, but only by pulling out all the intonational and gestural stops: *Why didn't you discard it? I d i s c á r d e d it! You just weren't paying attention!*

The most diabolical criminal we have ever rún across.[3]

God, did they cút them up!

With verbs like *donate, encounter,* and *slash* (without *up*) this cannot be done.

Freedom of order and freedom of accent. Where the value of phrasal verbs to the prosody of English stands out most clearly is in the coupling of accent and position. It retains something for English that the grammaticizing of word order might otherwise have destroyed: the freedom to put the transitive verb, or at least some significant part of it, at some other point than before its complement. Grammaticizing made it impossible to say *He the man ousted,* but with the phrasal verb there is no trouble with *He threw the man out.* At times it seems as if the verb proper and the particle had switched roles—the adverb becomes the verb and the verb the adverb:

They scratched the mistakes off. They offed (erased) the mistakes by scratching.

Johnny ran away. Johnny awayed (absented himself) by running.

This is particularly obvious when intransitive simple verbs become transitive phrasal verbs—the particle is what adds the transitive element:

They laughed (stared) him down. They downed him by laughing (staring).

In any case, the prosody benefits in that the important semantic feature, contained in *oust* or *out, erase* or *off,* and the like, can be put in the normal position for the nuclear accent. In a pair like

Discárd that old junk.

Throw that old junk awáy.

3. "Get Smart," television program, Boston, 23 August 1969.

where the junk has already been referred to, the one-word verb *discard* has to be put first, leaving the rest of the sentence to subside on a deflated intonational fall, while the two-word verb *throw away* gets the nuclear accent where it belongs, in the right position for the punch. There are other ways of doing this, for instance with the passive voice,

I want that old junk discárded.

but the phrasal verb does it more effectively because the element that can take end position is usually either a monosyllable such as *on, out, back, in, up, down,* or an iambic form like *around, about, along, aside, away, apart,* which enables the nuclear accent to fall on the very last syllable.

If this were merely a phonological question, determining nothing more in syntax than superficial choices of style, it might make possible the approach of some transformational grammarians who have treated shifts of accent and position as manifestations of an optional "particle movement." Presumably one has the option of saying *He put the money away* or *He put away the money,* the meaning being the same, but no option with *He put it away.* What makes a treatment purely in terms of conditioned variants attractive is this apparent lack of freedom of the pronoun along with the apparently negligible difference in meaning, much if not most of the time, between two sentences differing only by the position of the particle. But we have found that the pronoun is not so unfree as supposed, and we must now interpret why something like *Fancy taking on her* can be said, but rarely is.

It has been generally recognized that there is some connection between position and accent. For Kruisinga (§2209), "The chief cause of mid-position of noun objects is their want of stress," by which he explains the usual mid-position of nouns like *matter* and *thing:*

He took the matter up with the boss.

Let's talk things over.

Poutsma explains (p. 423) the mid-position of pronouns in the same way—they are "normally weak-stressed":

> I would rather wait him out, and starve him out than fight him out.
>
> We must make this up to you.

But this explanation fails to account for the mid-position of accented words,

> Let's take our friénds over.
>
> They shot the whole pláce up.

and says nothing about differences in meaning.

The late Peter Erades, echoing a similar view by Maria Schubiger, declared (p. 57) that "The principle governing the place of the objects . . . is neither stress nor length nor rhythm, but something quite different: the news value which the idea denoted by the object has in the sentence. Objects denoting ideas that have news value, no matter whether they are nouns or pronouns, long or short, have end-position; those that have no such value come between verb and adverb." Erades accounts thus for the frequent end position of nouns, especially of lengthily modified nouns which in the nature of the case are apt to have the most news value, and also for the normal mid-position of pronouns and "empty" nouns like *things, matter, business, stuff, subject*:

> ?He's bringing in the thíngs.
>
> He's bringing the things ín.
>
> He's bringing in the bággage.
>
> ?He brought up the súbject.
>
> He brought the subject úp.
>
> He brought up the divórce.

Erades's explanation also handles contexts in which a noun takes end position when first mentioned and mid position later. One of his examples:

> We'll make up a parcel for them . . . On the morning of Christmas Eve together we made the parcel up.

A similar one from Anna Hatcher:

There is [an easy way to clean spoons], if you haven't poured out the water in which you have boiled the egg.—I never pour the water out.[4]

These illustrate semantically empty nouns pulled away from the end. The opposite case is the so-called existential verb, which brings something on the scene. The name of that something would be expected, by Erades's account, to fall at the end. The archetypal verb of course is *there is:*

There was a misunderstanding.

In came the funniest-looking guy.

Around the corner is a police station.

And so for phrasal verbs:

It opens up unlimited opportunities.

It lets in a certain doubt.

He trotted out a bunch of old relics.

She picked out a new hat.

There is no need to labor the awkwardness of moving the noun leftward in these examples:

?It opens unlimited opportunities up.

It would appear that Erades is substantially confirmed. Yet in dismissing accent as a factor, he fails to keep it constant in his examples, which raises the suspicion that the effects he observed are due to something more than just the *position* of the noun. And he also overlooked the effect of the position of the particle; its change of position may be as important as that of the noun.

We can illustrate with an example which Poutsma (p. 421) thought was a lapse:[5]

Had she not so brought her child úp, and put her forth into the world?

Erades would say that the mid position of *child* is due to

4. Newspaper clipping, June 1957.
5. It went "against the evident purport of the sentence."

the child's having been mentioned before. But it is not necessary to shift positions to imply this—it can be done even more
unmistakably by leaving *child* on the end and de-accenting it:
    Had she not so brought úp her child?
In fact, this is exactly what would be necessary to get the
effect of previous mention if the verb were not a phrasal verb:
    Had she not so réared her child?
Unaccented end position of an item that is capable of being
accented is the most clearly redundant, the most unambiguously
repetitive of any combination of accent and position. The last
example fits that degree of redundancy. But if less is desired,
if *child* is meant to refer to something potentially new in the
context but at the same time not to be the semantic peak (that
importance being reserved for the verb), a phrasal verb provides the means for the distinction. This can be illustrated
by a modification of Poutsma's example. Imagine a school-
teacher whose respect for God and country has been called
into question. He replies in self-defense,
    That's exactly the way I'm bringing these chíldren úp.
in which *bring up* is the semantic peak but *children*[6] still con-

6. With its own *A* accent, or contour separation. For *A* accent, see
Bolinger, "A Theory of Pitch Accent in English," *Word* 14:142–143 (1958).
An *A* accent is an accentual highlighting achieved by an abrupt drop
in pitch from the syllable to be so highlighted. There may or may not
be a rise *to* the syllable in question, but more often than not there is.
Following is an example of two successive accents of which the first is
a *C* and the second is an *A*:

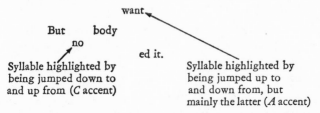

Syllable highlighted by
being jumped down to
and up from (*C* accent)

Syllable highlighted by
being jumped up to
and down from, but
mainly the latter (*A* accent)

For contour separation, see K. L. Pike, *The Intonation of American English*
(Ann Arbor, University of Michigan Press, 1945), p. 39.

veys new information. He also has the choice of treating *bring up* as redundant or otherwise uninformative and saying
    That's exactly the way I'm bringing these chíldren up.
In addition, the phrasal verb can do whatever the nonphrasal verb can do:
    That's exactly the way I'm bringing up these chíldren.
    That's exactly the way I'm rearing these chíldren.
    That's exactly the way I'm bringing úp these children.
    That's exactly the way I'm réaring these children.
—the first pair puts *children* at the semantic peak but leaves the verb unmarked as to redundancy; the second makes the verb the semantic peak but marks *children* as redundant.

I give another minimal pair, this time spotlighting the unaccented particle. In both sentences the noun gets the accent but in the first the verb (*to have on*) is redundant in that its semantic content has already been mentioned, while in the second it is new information:
    Was he wearing something to keep him warm?—Yes, he
      had a kind of short clóak on, and his legs were wrapped
      in coarse leggings that reached above his knees.
    Describe him.—Well, he was about six feet one, he had
      on a short clóak, and he walked with a slight stoop.
(It goes without saying that the first reply has both options, though with different implications; but the second would be difficult to reverse.)

The phrasal verb is not a case of optional or obligatory or stylistic hop and skip of the particle but is part of our means of achieving semantic focus. By putting the particle at the end and accenting it, we recapture the power to make the verb the high point without explicitly degrading anything else. By putting it there and not accenting it, we are able to make the verb explicitly redundant. In addition, nothing is sacrificed. The following set brings together the major contrasts:

How can they put Níxon over?
How can they put over Níxon?
How can they put Nixon óver?
How can they put óver Nixon?
How can they pút over Nixon?

The first occurs in a setting where acts of political maneuvering are familiar (*putting over* may or may not actually have been mentioned). The second and third approach the political maneuver from outside: they could be spoken by someone broaching the whole question of politics, the difference being in the relative newsworthiness of the person or the action. The fourth treats Nixon as redundant. The last is an instance of rectification—the accent displaced onto a syllable that would be meaningless if interpreted as highlighted in its own right implies "How can such things be?" "How can they be thinking of such a thing?"[7]

Contextual effects. The treatment of the prosody could terminate here, with the main outlines. But contextual effects are so subtle and so apt to be read as counter examples or as instances of some principle that has been neglected, that I find it necessary to carry the discussion a short way farther, into the domain of "style," perhaps, or "usage"—if such a distinction can be drawn.

First is the modification of outright redundancy into what might be termed "familiarity." If the noun retains the accent but the particle is put after it, the sensation most often seems to be just that of what is familiar or usual under the circumstances. In the first of the two following examples, the style of the family's breakfast makes it understood that the eggs

---

7. Here is an example in which accent on the verb proper is not meaningless in the verb's own right: *How did you blow up that big balloon?—I didn't. I púmped it up.*

will be boiled and that the act of taking them out is a matter of course; but in the second, the act of removing is essential to there being any eggs available—*take out* is like the bringing-on-the-scene or existential verbs cited earlier:

> What was wrong with breakfast this morning?—I forgot to take the éggs out. They got hard-boiled.

> Why isn't breakfast ready?—I forgot to take out the éggs. I'll have to wait until they're warm to boil them.

The familiarity or expectedness can be rather explicit, as when a familiar action is centered on an object that more or less entails the action, e.g. *cattle* entails *to drive, boat* entails *to sail, plane* entails *to pilot,* etc.:

> Where's Joe?—He's driving the cáttle in. He'll be along in a minute.

> Where's Joe?—He's sailing his bóat in. He'll be along in a minute.

(Contrast these with nonentailed verbs, where the unaccented particle is relatively less likely to take end position:

> He's bringing in the cáttle.

> He's hauling in his bóat.)

The semantic freight of the object—and the predictability of the action—is shown most dramatically by the speaker's freedom to front the item that carries the prime information:

> Where's Jack?—His sister—he's taking her out tonight.

Less usual would be

> Where's Jack?—?Some friends—he's taking them out tonight.

(The question mark preceding an expression indicates that it is doubtful but not necessarily unacceptable.) This same familiarity, the relative redundancy of the action once the identity of the noun is assumed, enables us to say

> Where's Jack?—He's taking his síster out tonight.

and makes it less likely that we will say

Where's Jack?—?He's taking out his síster tonight.
while
Where's Jack?—He's taking out some fríends tonight.
is perfectly normal. In either case we can do the opposite, but it is less likely and alters the balance of redundancy. Often the context offers no conspicuous clues, and we can only assume the ordinariness of certain actions and the familiarity of certain objects, as in the following:

It's almost ten o'clock. Put your níghtie on, now, and run up to bed.

I shouldn't think it would take you half an hour to do this small job.—Huh. It takes that long to put the tóols away.

It seems that the effect of lack of newsworthiness, hence of familiarity, noted by Erades is due not just to the shift of the accented noun away from the end but to the shift of the unaccented particle *to* the end. As in the last two examples, the noun remains the semantic peak but not in a "newness" sense, and the action is not contrastive at all.[8]

Second is what might be termed the suffusion of the sentence as a whole with a kind of relaxed rhetorical effect that comes from avoiding a terminal accent. It would be hard to say whether there is a causal relationship between this and the connotation of familiarity, but the result is clearly synergistic. This can be shown by its opposite, which is the shift of accent

8. The fact that end position of the particle is at the familiar end of the speech-level or register scale perhaps explains why until the present century end position was comparatively rare in writing. The formality of earlier literature kept the proportion of any kind of phrasal verb low (Konishi notes [p. 122] instances of self-correction on the part of writers, who replaced phrasal verbs with Latinate forms, e.g. Dryden, with *limited* for *bound up*, *introduced* for *brought in*), and the more familiar position by the same token would have been avoided with even more care. In *Pendennis* I found no instances of end position of the particle except with personal pronouns.

to the end in highly excited speech—a gee-whiz, look-what-we-have-here unexpectedness. I have many examples of distortions of normal stresses by this shift, for example, the remark made by a sports announcer,

Everything he looks at he'll photográph![9]
It is hard to imagine
Run the rascals óut!
said other than earnestly; not so with
Óust the rascals!
which can be offhand and humorous. If someone asks *How can I keep from being seen?* and we reply
How about pulling down the shádes?
the intent is probably serious or irritated. If we reply
How about pulling the shádes down?
there is a suggestion of relaxed irony; the solution was familiar and obvious.

Third, a variety of incidental effects can be produced by the play of accent and position on particular words. If instead of a highly definite term such as *Nixon* in the examples on page 55, we substitute a highly indefinite one such as *things,* the contextual possibilities are cut down. For one thing, no such importance can attach to this word as would justify giving it the accent, regardless of position:
*I have to clean thíngs up.
*I have to clean up thíngs.
Yet it can take the pre-accentual position (neutral as regards redundancy):
I have to clean things úp.
—this might be said by a housewife referring to the kitchen and dishware after a party—particular things, still newsworthy to some extent. If it comes at the end, with no accent, as in
I have to clean úp things.

9. Paramount, "Sports in Action," newsreel seen 19 March 1964.

it probably refers to things in the most general and redundant way—"I have to do cleaning"—as might be said by a cleaning woman to explain the kind of work she does. It is not necessary that the thing or person actually have been mentioned already in order to take the terminal de-accent. The following was a casual remark to a passerby made by a person who was preparing to clean the packed snow off his sidewalk:

Going to take óff a little of it.

The *little of it* was obvious from the situation, and by putting it where he did the speaker made his observation a commonplace greeting.

Fourth, where for reasons of contrast, emotional backshift, or whatever, the nuclear accent precedes both the particle and the object, the tendency is for terminal position not only to carry its own significance but to signal accent as well. In the following instance of emotional backshift it is assumed that there are no pitch, intensity, or duration contrasts after the nuclear accent:

Gíve
     up those pretensions.
Gíve
     those pretensions up.

We probably hear the accent on *pretensions* and *up* respectively. The same happens in

       did
   never
He   write up his report.

       did
   never
He   write his report up.

             thrown
          also
We gave it away, and we've   away at least a
  bushel.

thrown
also
We gave it away, and we've   at least a bushel
away.

Even a slight change in the prosodic variables after the accent can alter this.

There are cases, to be treated later (Chapter 10), where position has been stereotyped with particular meanings, and moving the particle is impossible without changing the meaning. Example:

He took off his hát and bówed.

He took his hát off and bówed.

In the first, the action of removal is a gesture: *take off = doff*. In the second, the hat is perhaps removed for fear it may fall off in the act of bowing.

CHAPTER 5

The Definite-Noun-Phrase Test

Nature of the test. The diagnostic frame introduced as Test 8 (see Chapter 1), which discriminates transitive phrasal verbs from transitive combinations that are not phrasal verbs, can now be discussed with the benefit of what has been said about phrasal-verb prosody. The following, for example, appear to be equivalent pairs:

They took along a couple of old newspapers.
They took with them a couple of old newspapers.
They set aside a few barrels.
They set to one side a few barrels.
They brought forward several new recruits.
They brought frontward several new recruits.

Yet in another context it is apparent that they are not:

They took along the newspapers.
*They took with them the newspapers.
They set aside the barrels.
*They set to one side the barrels.
They brought forward the recruits.
*They brought frontward the recruits.

The frame is defined as a simple definite noun phrase consisting of either just a single proper noun (its most drastic form) or of *the* plus an unmodified common noun. The latter, in the terminology of a recent dissertation on the article, is "anaphoric *the*" as distinguished from "determinative *the*."[1] Determinative *the,* as in the third of the following examples,

---

1. Beverly Levin Robbins, "The Definite Article in Logic and Grammar," Ph. D. diss., University of Pennsylvania, 1965. Abstract in *Linguistics* 40:35–36 (1968).

is not a test:

He pushed in the key.

*He pushed inward the key.

He pushed inward the right-hand key.

—with added modifiers, a definite noun phrase of whatever type becomes acceptable following many adverbs besides the ones that form phrasal verbs. The test—with anaphoric *the*—has been used rather generally, though with no attempt to justify it, so far as I am aware. Palmer stars the example

*He ordered about the men (p. 187).

and one wonders whether he would agree that no star is called for if the example is changed to

You may order about whatever men you think need ordering about.

Yet he is right in ignoring examples like this. The first explanation that offers itself is the principle of longest element last, and if we try this again on Palmer's example,

He ordered about the men in uniform.

it seems to work. But a little experimenting shows it to be largely false. Palmer's example is inserviceable for American English.[2] I replace it with two synonyms of *to repeat: to do*

2. Though apparently no similar retreat is registered in British English, in American English *about* is being crowded out by *around*. Stereotyped phrasal verbs are still common with *about:*

That brought about the revolution.

It came about that all the losses were sustained by one side.

But in the literal sense *about* is being more and more restricted to formal usage. The following are normal for me:

He stalked about the place for an hour or two and then left.

She tiptoed about the room, being careful not to wake anyone.

Around would make the first action seem one of low rather than high dudgeon and the second to be aimless. When the action per se is relatively relaxed and unpurposive, *about* is not normal:

?He walked about the property.

?They strolled about the park.

The old-fashioned *to gad about* can be compared with the more recent *to bum around*. Both the phrasal verbs based on *about* and nominal compounds based on those phrasal verbs have a certain formality or quaintness:

over and *to do again.* Both have the same number of syllables, but one is a phrasal verb and the other is not:

You must do over the job.

*You must do again the job.[3]

Evidently phonetic bulk is not the primary explanation. What counts most is the meaning of the definite noun phrase.

To illustrate, I use three synonymous expressions: *to telephone, to call up,* and *to get (someone) on the phone.* Imagine a conversation into which the referent of *John* has already been introduced, and the question has to do with the means of getting some information from him. Suppose also that although "John" has been introduced, his connection with the question is still newsworthy. This allows two possibilities. We can say

Why don't you call John úp?

Why don't you get John on the phóne?

but we cannot say

Why don't you telephone Jóhn?

because the point of the question is not "John" but the means of reaching him. Nor can we say

Why don't you télephone John?

de-accenting *John,* because the condition was that "John" was not to be that redundant. If the verb *telephone* is to be used at all, it is necessary to mention *John* in some other way, perhaps by adding another sentence:

If you have to reach John why don't you télephone him?

---

to busy oneself about (the kitchen), to bandy about, turnabout, runabout (contrast *runaround*), *gadabout, roustabout.* The use of the two together is also fading (*Round about them orchards sweep*) though it survives in the adjective *roundabout.* The foregoing explains the need to modify Palmer's example:

*Stop ordering about my friends!

Stop ordering around my friends!

3. The stress pattern is not a factor. There are more particles with the pattern of *again* than with that of *over.*

Again, suppose a conversation in which "John" is the point of the question. Now it is not the verb *to telephone* but the phrase *to get (someone) on the phone* that is in difficulties:

Why don't you telephone Jóhn?
Why don't you call up Jóhn?
*Why don't you get on the phone Jóhn?

If *on the phone* is to appear at all as a newsworthy item, it must be handled as *John* was in the first situation, by giving it a separate nuclear unit:

Why don't you get Jóhn? On the phone, I mean.

Elsewhere than with the definite noun phrase, all three possibilities are open:

Why don't you telephone somebody who knows something about it?
Why don't you call up somebody who knows something about it?
Why don't you get on the phone somebody who knows something about it?

These examples show that an adverbial adjunct to a verb is not normally allowed to precede a simple definite object noun phrase. The exceptions—the phrases that behave like simple verbs in this respect—are defined as phrasal verbs.

Rationale of the test. The restrictions are explained by two principles: grammaticization, and Erades's newsworthiness. The first requires SVO order in

You must repeat the job.
*You must the job repeat.

regardless of the newsworthiness of *the job.* The second—the broader of the two principles—requires that the less newsworthy item take interior position. A definite noun phrase is by definition redundant as to semantic content; its usual function is anaphoric, to relate to previous mention, not to give new information.[4] This is not true of an adverbial adjunct, which accordingly is given end position:

You'll have to do the job again (well, tomorrow, acceptably).

*You'll have to do again (etc.) the job.

With noun phrases other than the ones described, there is no longer the restrictive semantic redundancy and position becomes free again. We are now outside the test frame. So for indefinite determiners:

*He has left to one side the problem.

He has left to one side a problem. It is this . . .

*Pull separately the blinds.

Pull separately all the blinds.

*They brought to the victims.

They weren't able to bring to even one of the suffocation victims that had been hastily dragged out of the burning building.

?It snowed under the students.

That would snow under any student.[5]

Also for definte noun phrases with post-modifiers:

*He said again the words.

He said again (again and again, softly, today) the words that meant so much to him.

In the phrasal verb the particle is not bound by these restric-

---

4. It is not always anaphoric. The phrase *the dead* refers to people who are dead, whether or not mentioned within the previous context. Superlatives are common in the same way. With this meaning the definite-noun-phrase test does not serve; one can readily find

It's enough to bring alive the dead.

His wrath would turn helpless the strongest.

We would probably not regard *bring alive,* and certainly not *turn helpless,* as a phrasal verb.

5. As indicated on p. 20, the problem here may not be the fact that *to bring to* and *to snow under* are not phrasal verbs but that without a predisposing context *to* and *under* are too suggestive of prepositions.

tions. It can link to its verb in the manner of a one-word unit:

Pull down the blinds.

Write off the losses.

Bring along Gwen.

Bring aboard the cargo.

Or it can follow the object in the manner of an ordinary adverb:

Pull the blinds down.

Write the losses off.

Bring Gwen along.

Bring the cargo aboard.

Phonetic bulk may wield a secondary influence: "It is beyond doubt that the length as well as the complexity of the complement is an important factor" (Fairclough, p. 62). The longer an element is, the more likely it is to contain critical information and hence to take the normal position for semantic focus, at the end. This is an invitation to speakers to reinterpret the data: if long elements are usually encountered at the end, the end will appear to be the place where long elements belong. Another explanation is possible: end position is normal for both longer elements and semantic focus, and speakers adjust the competing forces as best they can, favoring semantic focus and using the referential system (especially pronouns) to get certain long elements out of the way. In any case, examples like

*You'll never be able to treat separately John.

You'll never be able to treat separately John Aloysius Jones. point to a factor of length. (Again, even here there may be a matter of previous mention. We are likely to refer to a person by his full name only if he is just being introduced to the context, or we are so pretending.)

CHAPTER 6

Particles Other Than Adverbs

When a particle changes its position, is the effect only prosodic or are other relationships in the sentence altered? We have seen dual functions when the particle served as an adprep: it belonged both to the verb as adverb and to the noun as preposition:

They walked through the house.

An analogous question is whether the particle can belong to the verb as adverb and to the noun as quasi-adjective, and what role in phrasal verbs may actually be played by lexical adjectives.

Adverbial particles that resemble adjectives. Again it was Peter Erades who hinted at the kinship. He observed (p. 59) that in

She pushed the basin across.

the particle is "a predicative rather than an adverbial adjunct." An example already used can be cited again,

He ran the flag up.

—after the flag has been run up it is up, just as after the basin has been pushed across it is across. Spasov speaks of verbs that "assume resultative sense" under these conditions (p. 47). The fact that the particle can assume the *position* of a predicative adjunct is in itself suspicious and our suspicions are confirmed when we find particles in predicative position that are synonymous with adjectives:

He knocked the man out.
He knocked the man cold.
He knocked them apart.
He knocked them loose.

They let him off.
They set him free.
Wipe those tools off.
Wipe those tools clean.

Intransitive verbs show just as clearly the tendency for the adverb to attach itself semantically to the noun, in this case the noun subject. As part of this process, some intransitives become copula-like:

He stood apart. (He took a position to one side.)
He stood apart. (He *was* in a position to one side.)[1]
He stands out. (He *is* out, is conspicuous.)

Other examples of intransitives with subjective complements:

He went out of his mind.
He went crazy.
The money ran out.
The money ran short.
The trap door dropped to.
The trap door dropped shut.
It came apart. It came off.
It came undone. It came loose.[2]
He got away.
He got free.

Furthermore, at least some conjunctions between particles and adjectives are perfectly normal:

He held the gun out and ready.
With a bound he was away and free.

And the particles in question are freely used as predicates of *be*, both in adverb-adprep function:

Have they made it to the other side of the mountain, do

---

1. An even better analog for *apart* is this from *Rob Roy*, p. 226: *pushing us separate from each other*.

2. The fact of stereotyping is evident in the restriction of this particular set to non-Latin forms. In place of *undone* and *loose* we can have *untied* and *unfastened* but not *detached* nor *disconnected*.

you think?—They must surely be over (the mountain)
by now.

The train must be approaching the station.—Isn't it already
past (the station)?

and as what some dictionaries class as adjectives—in any case,
frequently having nearly synonymous adjectives or past
participles:

The meeting is over. (terminated)

School is out. (dismissed)

His term is up. (finished)

The reports are in. (received)[3]

He's around. (close)

She's well off.[4]

Adjectives that behave like adverbial particles. The link between particle and adjective would be complete if we could
find verb-adjective combinations that pass the definite-noun-

3. Or more properly, as pointed out by L. A. Hill, p. 81, in connection
with *send in* (a resignation), *put in* (a claim), and *call in* (the books),
the meaning of "in" is "in the hands of the proper person or authority."

4. It cannot be argued, I think, as in Fraser, p. 78, that the possibility
of predication with *be* counts against viewing the word as a particle and
the combination as a phrasal verb. To do so would mean that in a sentence
like

In bad weather they let out school early.

let out is not a phrasal verb because *School's out!* is a normal sentence.
It is better to follow Fairclough, p. 167, who feels that the commutability
of the verbs in sentences like

Wormold got up early. Wormold was up early.

The dividend went up. The dividend is up.

"is the strongest justification for including *be*-P among the class of phrasal
verbs." The same extended meanings of the particles can be found with
be as with other verbs, for example perfectivity in *The game is up* (Fairclough, p. 167).

The analogy between particles and past participles is so strong that
over, for example, is able to pick up a *with* that is extended analogically
through a chain of synonyms:

They finished with their work.

They got their work finished with.

They got their work done with.

They got their work over with.

phrase test. In general they do not:

He knocked the man unconscious. *He knocked unconscious the man.

It left the class perplexed. *It left perplexed the class.

They painted their door blue. *They painted blue their door.[5]

But some do:

Let the prisoners loose. Let loose the prisoners.

They cut the speech short. They cut short the speech.

Break the cask open. Break open the cask.

And those that do, reveal the same prosodic features as are found in phrasal verbs with particles. The play of accent and position are the same in

I forgot to cut the mélon open. I forgot to cut open the mélon.

I forgot to take the éggs out. I forgot to take out the éggs.

Likewise the same semantic spreading-out. We noted that the semantic feature of *oust* was postposed onto the particle in *to throw out,* as if in *to throw out* the roles of semantic head and semantic satellite were reversed: *to throw out* = "to oust by throwing." Similarly *to cut open* = "to open by cutting," *to chop free* = "to free by chopping," etc. This altered balance of semantic content is more evident with semantically empty causative verbs. We can compare *make* + adjective with *get* + particle:

They got out the report = They issued (outed) the report.

---

5. The last example is from Randolph Quirk and Jan Svartvik, *Investigating Linguistic Acceptability* (The Hague, Mouton, 1965). They give (p. 107) the following figures from their acceptability tests, revealing the special character of *open:*

	acceptable	question	unacceptable
They pushed the gate open.	73	3	0
He pushed open the door.	60	13	3
You painted your fence blue.	72	3	1
They painted blue their door.	4	14	58

We got in the obituary all right; there was still space for it = We inserted (inned) the obituary.

They made ready the plans = They readied the plans.

He made clear the intention = He clarified the intention.

They made public the news = They publicized the news.[6]

The relationship between verb and particle that Erades saw as a predicative adjunct and Spasov calls resultative, and which I have here likened to a causative, has been formalized by Fairclough in a forthcoming article. He writes (private communication), "I would regard *carry underground, bend inwards* as involving a (causative) embedding deep structure, together with the less problematic *send down* (*a sandwich*) and *send* (*James*) *to Newgate*. This would seem to establish the intuitively desirable identity of deep structure between such cases and V[erb] + Comp[lement] forms like *make* (*James*) *happy.* . . ."

Adjectives as particles. There seems little question that at least some adjectives are entitled to be classed with the particles that are used in phrasal verbs. But how many of them? The adverbial particles are drawn from a very small if not a closed set: they are the adverbs of motion and terminus plus a few close analogs (*on board,* for example, as well as *aboard*). Adjectives are an open set. So it is to be expected, given the fact that not all adjectives behave like particles, that there must be some explanation for the ones that do.

The theory I offer is based on the identification of three

6. Similarly with inceptives: *to flush red* = "To redden by flushing," *to turn red* = "to redden." There are other such empty verbs whose only function seems to be to spread out the semantic content. For example, *set: to set apart* = "to separate"; *to set afire* = "to ignite"; *to set alight* = "to light"; *to set free* = "to free". There are, of course, stereotypes like *to set down* "to record," *to set out* "to display," in which the meaning of the whole is not so readily identified with just the meaning of the complement.

sets of adjective phrasal verbs and a comparison of two of them. Synonymy plays a role in all three, which suggests that the classes are semantic and therefore at least partially open, whether on the side of the verb or of the adjective or both.

The first set consists of an empty causative verb—*make* and occasionally one of its synonyms, for example, *keep, leave, have, hold,* and *render*—with an indefinite, but probably not large, group of adjectives:

It leaves obvious the mistakes.

He made known the facts.

It renders necessary the measures.

It makes possible the result.

It makes plain the purpose.

The adjective *ready* combines more freely with all these verbs than do most other adjectives:

Have (make, hold, leave, keep) ready the answers.

The meaning of the set coincides with that of the existential verbs noted earlier: it is uniformly "to present, reveal, bring on the scene." Where the existential sense fades, the result is less acceptable; thus a command with *have ready* more clearly means "to present" than do other forms of the verb:

Have ready the answers.

Be sure to have ready the answers.

*They all had ready the answers.

This explains why definite noun phrases have no trouble coming at the end: *It makes plain the purpose* is the same as *It brings out the purpose,* while *It makes happy the children* is unrelated to an existential notion, and is unacceptable.[7] It also explains the curious phrasal verb *to make good* (to restore,

7. But Thackeray's *A man may do worse than make happy two of the best creatures in the world* (*Pendennis,* p. 335) is normal for the reasons already noted.

bring back on the scene):

He made good the loss.[8]

It does not of course explain the use of *good* in this sense, nor does it account for the idiomatic cast of all such phrases: we can only say that the formation of a phrasal verb along these lines is facilitated, but once formed it is self-perpetuating, like any idiom. Composability is relative. (Nor does the idiomaticity of a verb-adjective combination infallibly lead to its becoming a phrasal verb. *To learn cold* is certainly idiomatic, yet

He learned the formula cold.

*He learned cold the formula.)

The second set is the opposite—it is relatively closed on the adjective side but almost completely open on the verb side. It is here that we find conditions closest to those of the ordinary phrasal verbs: a very few particles making a large number of combinations. I have identified four adjectives—again partially synonymous in a significant way—two of which, *open* and *loose,* are about as freely composable as any particle, with the two others, *free* and *clear,* not far behind:

I held open the door, left open the hatch, pushed open the window, smashed open the bottle, sneaked open the purse, pricked open the balloon, banged open the can.

I raked (swept, shoveled, plowed, flushed) open the path; it was clogged with leaves (snow).

He pried loose the lid, shook loose the bonds, wrestled loose the bolts, cast loose the lines.

8. What relationship if any the meaning "to secure" has to existential verbs—perhaps "to keep on the scene"—I am unable to say, but there are combinations with *make* that carry it: *to make safe, to make secure, to make good* (it has or had this sense), and *to make fast* all allow to some extent the postposition of the definite noun phrase: *They made safe the locks, made fast the lines.*

I worked free the wheel, shook free the cover, pulled free the robe, gouged free the opening.

It blew clear the road, harrowed clear the field, sifted clear the sand.[9]

The third set is lexically open but semantically closed. It would be impossible—short of doing a complete dictionary—to list either the verbs or the adjectives. But the semantic relationship between the two is circumscribed. Compare:

Will it bleach white the undies?

*Will it paint white the fence?

Bleach and *white* are synonymous, or represent some kind of cause-effect relationship in which the effect is more or less intrinsic to the cause: to bleach something is to make it white. To paint something, however, does not in any way imply whiteness. Other examples:

He's planing (buffing, sanding) smooth the boards.

Why do you plane (buff, sand) the boards?—*Because it leaves smooth the surface.

I was busy downstairs wringing dry the sheets.

?I was busy downstairs squeezing dry the sheets.

He was under the car screwing tight the bolts.

---

9. The following, which appeared after this material was written, gives independent confirmation of the notions expressed here: "Forming a group of its own are certain sentences that have the same structure as the phrasal verb; they can be submitted to the same tests of position and replacement as the phrasal verb, though they are different from it in the sense that they have, instead of an adverbial particle, an adjective:

He tore the envelope open.
He tore open the envelope he had received.
He tore it open.
That loss would set Charles free.
That loss would set free all the feelings he had for her.
That loss would set them free."

Mario Zamudio, "On Defining the Phrasal Verb: Its Grammatical Structure and Its Recognition," *Revista de Lingüística Aplicada* (Universidad de Concepción, Chile) 7:42 (1969).

*He was under the car turning tight the bolts. ("He was under the car turning up the bolts" is acceptable.)

They packed tight the wadding.

*They packed loose the wadding.

They cut short the interview.

*They made short the interview.

He whittled short the stalk.

*He chewed short the stalk.

She was down on her hands and knees scrubbing clean the floor.

*You can't just wish clean the floor!

I sprained my arm banging empty the cans yesterday.

*The trash collectors left empty the cans.

I drained dry the glass.

*I poured dry the glass.

He pounded soft the clay.

*He worked soft the clay.

It ironed flat the foil.

*It threw flat the foil.

The starred examples are all normal with the adjective postposed:

It leaves the surface smooth.

I was squeezing the sheets dry.

He was turning the bolts tight.

They packed the wadding loose.

They made the interview short.

He chewed the stalk short.

You can't just wish the floor clean!

The trash collectors left the cans empty.

I poured the glass dry.

He worked the clay soft.

It threw the foil flat.

It is clear, therefore, that mere causativeness is not the explanation: all these verbs are causative.[10] It is causativeness plus intrinsic consequence, a kind of semantic cognate object. Consider the causative verb *turn*. In its general sense, it does not pass the definite-noun-phrase test:

*It turns black the banana.

*It turned young the man.

But *turn* has the specific sense "to sour,"[11] and when used causatively in this sense, it passes the test:

It turned sour the milk.

Idiomaticity is a factor here as in the previous set. Many theoretically possible combinations are not acceptable. A curious example is that of extension—it is normal for width but not for length:

They stretched (pulled, spread, drew) wide the fabric.

*They stretched (pulled, drew) long the rope.

Idiomaticity affects the combinations at a higher level, also: some redundancies are unacceptable regardless of order—the role of learnèd forms should be investigated here:

*It reduces the material short (small, narrow).

(Compare the earlier examples *reduce down* as against *diminish down*.) On the other hand, again as in the previous set, idiomaticity does not of itself make these combinations phrasal verbs. *To bleed white* is an idiom, but

They bled the victims white.

*They bled white the victims.

There are assuredly dialectal preferences among the examples I have given; some of the examples may be differently judged by different people, but probably not in violation of the general

10. A point that needs investigating is whether of the causative verbs those which *create* the object are excluded. This is the classical "affect-effect" contrast; see Charles J. Fillmore, "The Case for Case," in Bach and Harms, eds., *Universals in Linguistic Theory*, p. 4.

11. *Webster's Third New International*, definition 6a (2).

principle: for a speaker unfamiliar with *to turn* "to sour," the example *It turned sour the milk* will probably be as unacceptable as *It turns black the banana*. There are also differences of register. The following examples are good literary sentences, but doubtful colloquial ones:

Hold high the banners.
Open wide the doors.
Sink deep the wells.
He set alight the stars.

Comparing the second and the third sets, we find reason to suspect that one is a special case of the other. The adjectives *open, loose, free,* and *clear* are, as was pointed out, roughly synonymous. They all signify "disconnected" in some sense. Disconnectedness can be a natural result of almost any vigorous action. Consequently these adjectives can be used with a wide variety of verbs, precisely in terms of the causative pattern just described. Where the pattern is not satisfied, the combination is less likely, though *open* and *loose* are still possible:

I'm going to try to get open the window.
I wanted to get at the contents, but it was no use; I couldn't get loose the lid.
The fairy charmed the prince free. *The fairy charmed free the prince.
*Use both wipers to see if you can't get clear the windows. ("Wipe clear" is acceptable.)

Of the four adjectives, *open* has come most to resemble an adverbial particle. Its combinations to some extent transcend the semantic restrictions on the other adjectives:

He waved open the door and we walked in.
He held open the gate for us.

—but are still subject to them:

He jiggled open the door.
*They declared open the season.

The rather special status of *open* can also be seen in the readiness with which it can be used before unmodified nouns, where other adjectives tend to be avoided because of ambiguity:

He pushes open doors.

*He's planing smooth boards.

*I was banging empty cans.

?It cuts short conversations.

*It pounds soft clay.

*He always makes good losses.

*It's always wise to make clear intentions.

In certain of their combinations, *loose* and *free* can precede an unmodified noun; thus *turn loose* and *let free* are cohesive enough as units to allow this:

Do you always make a habit of letting loose (turning free) prisoners?

There is possibly a phonological factor here also, though it is extremely difficult to test separately from that of ambiguity. The avoidance of successive accents leads to certain rearrangements and interpolations of unaccented syllables (*kind of a, so good of a, half a: half an hour* rather than *a half hour*).[12] The unaccented syllable in *open* gives it an advantage over *loose, free,* and *clear.* One can perhaps test with proper names:

When they cut open John, guess what they found in place of a heart.

?I wish I could find a conversationalist who could cut short John!

?If they aren't willing to release the other prisoners, they might at least let loose John!

Whether to ease the accent situation or to avoid ambiguity, an oblique case may be resorted to:

They might at least let loose of John.

12. See my "Pitch Accent and Sentence Rhythm," in Bolinger, *Forms of English* (Cambridge, Harvard University Press, 1965), pp. 145–155.

He always makes good on losses.

With adverbial particles there is no problem either of ambiguity or of accent:

It takes more than that to hold back John.

Infinitives. If adjectives can be found behaving like adverbial particles in the make-up of phrasal verbs, the question naturally arises whether other lexical categories may be involved as well. I have no clear examples of nouns, though if the definite-noun-phrase test is suspended it is easy to invent examples with objective complements that resemble phrasal verbs:

*They elected president Andrew Johnson.

Do you think the American people will elect president any weasel-worded, mealy-mouthed scamp who projects a personality on a TV screen?

(This is reminiscent of the Reed and Kellogg treatment of *They made Victoria queen* as equivalent to *They made-queen Victoria.*[13])

A few infinitives, however, have wedged themselves into the phrasal-verb pattern. The most numerous family is with *let,* of which the *NED* lists *let be, let fall, let go, let pass, let run,* and *let slip.* We can add *let fly.* The kinship with phrasal verbs in which *let* combines instead with an adverb or an adjective can be seen in the following:

He let go the lines. (Compare "He let loose the lines.")

He let go a blast. (Compare "He let out a blast.")

He let fly an oath. (Compare "He let out an oath.")

He let fall the remark.

He let slip the opportunity.

The similarity between *let loose* and *let go* is evident in what happens in the dialects—both add *of:*

He let go of the lines.

13. Alonzo Reed and Brainerd Kellogg, *Higher Lessons in English* (New York, C. E. Merrill Co., 1906), 54.

He let loose of the lines.

With *let go* there is probably a prosodic factor:

Let go (of) my leg!

Let go of John!

But there is also a semantic bifurcation:

Let go of him! (Release him from your grasp.)

Let him go! (Don't detain him.)

In addition to those with *let*, there are at least two combinations with *make: make believe* and *make do*. They match two different senses of the phrasal verb *make out:*

They made believe that they were our friends = They made out that they were our friends.

They made do with what they had = They made out with what they had.

The phrasal verbs embodying infinitives are highly stereotyped. One is not free, I think, to coin the likes of

?He let ride (slide) the remark.

?He let rise the doubt.

—though *Let it ride* and *Let it slide* are familiar stereotypes in their own right.

Other particles. A thorough study of the lexicon will doubtless reveal other kinds of particles in addition to adverbs, adjectives, and infinitives. A marginal type has already been mentioned in which a preposition, generally *to,* is followed by an unmodified noun:

It brings to light the facts.

I took to heart the advice.

It brings to mind the dangers.

Keep in mind the alternatives

When I asked you not to make that noise I had in mind the neighbors.

They took on board the cargo.

They brought up front the actors.

These seem to be relatively few and limited to verbs like *bring,* *take,* and *have,* and also to nouns which in combination with those verbs suggest the equivalent of an existential phrasal verb: they are again expressions that bring something on the scene, fix it in consciousness. Other combinations fail:

*He brought to heel the dog.

*It brought to bay the wolves.

*She talks to death her friends.

*They are holding in trust the bonds.

All these combinations are highly stereotyped. There is no freedom to coin even in conformity with the semantic restrictions on phrasal verbs in general and existential verbs in particular:

*It brings to fruition the efforts.

*They put on display the merchandise.

Summary. With the comparison of adjectives and particles I hope to have shown two things: that at least some adjectives most of the time, and a great many adjectives part of the time, can be used in combinations that are functionally identical to phrasal verbs; and that this identity proves the rightness of Erades's intuition that the particles may modify nouns. I would go a step farther and say that this is the normal situation with phrasal verbs: they denote an action and at the same time a result. When we say *He ran up the flag* or *He ran the flag up* we are saying both that he ran the flag in an upwise direction and that as a result the flag was up. In addition, the first of these two senses embodies within the particle a verbal feature—we are free to interpret *to press down* as "to press in a downward direction" or "to down by pressing." The same is true with adjectives: *to push open* is "to push toward an open position" or "to open by pushing." And with infinitives the particle element is explicitly a verb: *to let him go* is "to let (release) him + he goes," as *to push it open is* "to push it + it is open." No matter what class the particle comes from, the semantic features are joined as they are in prefixed derivatives whether Germanic or Latin or other: *to upraise, to backshift, to incline,* to *extrapose,* and so on.[14]

Though the phrasal verb embodies both the action and the result, the position of the particle tends to make one or the other paramount. With transitive verbs, when the particle is postposed it tends to modify the noun; when it stands next to the verb it behaves more like a verbal affix. Much of the time there is no practical difference—if there were, the prosodic nuances would have to be sacrificed. One case where the affinities are kept fairly clear is with *get* and *make:*

Get in that report. (deliver it)
Get that report in. (delivered)
He's getting out a paper. (publishing)
We'd better get this paper out. (issued)
They made clear their intentions. (clarified)
They made their intentions clear. (unmistakable)
They made public the bad news. (publicized)
They made the bad news public. (common knowledge)
He knocked out Joe Frazier. (defeated)
He knocked Joe Frazier out. (unconscious)
They got the man off. (acquitted)
Get the agony over. (finished)

Mostly the contrary inclinations reveal themselves in more subtle ways. In the following,

14. As is well known, the prefixed derivatives have extended their meanings much more radically, to the point that the Germanic ones are often less "literal" than their Latin counterparts: one may either *uphold* or *sustain* a veto, but a support may only *sustain,* not *uphold,* a roof—here *sustain* is like *hold up.* Similarly with *uplift* and *elevate,* with deverbals such as *outgrowth* and *excrescence.*

> What are you tearing up that paper for?—To use as packing around the china.
>
> What are you tearing that paper up for?—To keep him from reading it.

the second suggests that the purpose is to *have* the paper in a torn and illegible state; the first is indifferent to this—whole paper and torn paper may be used together. If in the following,

> He pushed open the door. He pushed the door open.
>
> ?He pushed shut the door. He pushed the door shut.

we find *push shut* a little less likely than *push open* by comparison with *push X shut* and *push X open,* both of which are good, this probably reflects the purpose of the actions. To push something shut is generally to *have* it shut; to push it open is as likely to be for the purpose of getting through, not necessarily to have the thing in an open state. With

> He pushed open the door and went in.
>
> He pushed the door open and went in.

we have the sensation of an uninterrupted succession in the first, while the second would be appropriate if after opening the door he stood back a moment and then went in—the open state has some importance in its own right. In

> Don't scuff your shoes.
>
> Don't scuff up your shoes.
>
> Don't scuff your shoes up.

the first refers only to the action, while the second and third both refer to the effect on the shoes, with the latter making the effect most explicit. The dual affinity of adverbs—verb-modifying and noun-modifying—is not confined to phrasal verbs. In

> If you think he is fat, you haven't looked at him sideways.
>
> If you think he is fat, you haven't looked at him sidewise.

sideways refers not only to the manner of looking but to the position of "him," who is standing sideways to the observer.

Sidewise is a bit absurd because it refers only to the manner of looking. In

She put the dress on backwards.

She took the dress off backwards.

the first can refer either to the manner or the resulting position, but the second can refer only to the manner.

CHAPTER 7

Semantic Features of the Particles

The importance of resultant condition suggests a hypothesis about the nature of the adverbial particles that may form part of a phrasal verb. I offer this: In its core meaning (though not necessarily in the figurative extensions discussed in Chapters 9 and 10) the particle must contain two features, one of motion-through-location, the other of terminus or result. This excludes manner and time adverbials, which contain neither:

*He built well the fire.
*She stitched carefully the rip.
*I bought yesterday the stocks.

(All are acceptable with *up*.) It excludes place and stance adverbials that give result but not motion:

*We brought here the bags.
*I left home the money.
*She crooked akimbo her arms.
?He set afire the house.

(Compare *I brought home the money,* where *home* means "to home" rather than "at home," and the phrasal verbs *leave in* and *leave out* which seem to function as negatives of *take out* and *put in,* that is, to mean respectively "not to take out" and "not to put in." Compare also the marginal *behind* in *I left behind the keys,* in which motion away shrinks "behind" as if to a kind of reverse terminus, with *I threw behind the keys,* in which "behind" is only a direction.) It excludes direction adverbials that give motion but not result:

*He tossed upward the ball.

*They pulled downward the blinds.[1]

It also perhaps explains why *near*, although it may be an adprep, for example,

They drew near the shore = They drew near near the shore = They drew near to the shore.

does not function as a particle:

They brought the chair near.

*They brought near the chair.

The reason, I suspect, is that the "motion" component is absent and has to be supplied by the verb: *draw near* contains it, but

They walked near the shore.

refers to location, not approach.[2] Finally, it explains the inclusion of a few two-word "particles" in which the functions

---

1. The most telling counter-example I have is from Anna Hatcher (personal communication, June 1957). She overheard the following, from a speaker who had undertaken to repair an old rug that was getting threadbare in two spots; presumably the speaker pointed as she said "I wove back and forth this . . . ," and implied "but the other spot would have been too difficult." It strikes me that without the *deixis ad oculos*, which is about as far as one can go in contrastive pointing, sentences like

*I wove back and forth the fabric.

*I sewed in and out the worn spot.

*I stitched inward the tear.

are unacceptable. It is only the extraordinarily strong contrast that is able to force a terminal position after an adverb that contains no trace of resultant condition.

Poetic license admits *He hurled heavenward his plaint*. The *-ward* words are a peculiar set. Mostly they do not enter phrasal verbs, but *forward* is an exception; perhaps helped by nautical usage it has come to denote a resultant state: *They pushed forward the recruits*, *They pushed backward (frontward) the recruits*.

2. *Near* may also be influenced by its antonym *far*, which cannot even be an adprep. Ultimately all these conditions facilitate but do not necessarily predict a given combination. Phrasal verbs belong to the lexicon, and while the conditions for creating one may be highly favorable it may or may not actually be created. Syntactic combinations involve rules that are applied at will, and the results are not entered in the lexicon: *high scaffolding, from Chicago, comfortably arranged* contain almost perfectly demountable parts. Creating a new item in the lexicon involves analogies. If they are sufficient and sufficiently strong, the analogical extension will probably be made. Otherwise it may or may not be. *Near* happens to be marginal.

are divided: a preposition embodies the motion feature, an unmodified noun the terminus feature. This is best illustrated by the forms which still show a trace of the divided functions: *abroad, ashore, astern,* and others with the prepositional *a-* prefix. One, *aboard,* still alternates with its unreduced congener:

They brought on board the passengers.

They brought aboard the passengers.

Others are listed on pp. 80–81.

A particle may be used in combinations where the terminus-result feature is absent. This would be generally true of transitive verbs whose object has been deleted. Thus *Sit down* and *Chop down the tree* are different from

You'll never make a dent that way! Chop down!

in which *down = downward.* Only a direction is given, and no result is implied. I would not regard this *chop down* as a phrasal verb. (It is barely possible to find a particle used in this way with a transitive verb whose object has not been deleted:

You'll never succeed that way! Chop the limb off dówn!

—again = downward.)

As with the example using *home,* it can happen that the same adverb sometimes meets the conditions of the hypothesis and sometimes not. An example with *along* was cited earlier: **They sat along drowsily the paths in the park* (as against *They strolled along drowsily the paths in the park*)—*along* was excluded as a pure preposition, but then pure prepositions lack, as a class, the feature of motion. Many of the particles which do contain the feature and are usable in phrasal verbs are precisely the ones that appear as quasi-verbs in the imperative:

Out!   *With!
Back!   *To!

Away with you!   *Toward!
Down, Fido!
Over!
Head up!
Toes out!

or as a virtual verb in the now antiquated
We must away.

There are also the ones that appear with nonstative *be*:
Be off with you!
I'll be right up.—See that you *do*. (Compare "I'll be ready
in a minute.—See that you *are*.")

And we find among other particles a cognate relationship to
verbs:
They brought together the tribes. They gathered the tribes.
They cut asunder the bonds. They sundered the bonds.
He split apart the log. He parted the log.

An example of a particle which is not an adprep (hence not
a preposition) but which may again either satisfy or not satisfy
the conditions of the hypothesis is *astern*:
They pulled astern the dory.

This is acceptable if it means where the dory came to be as
a result of the pulling. It is unacceptable if it means where
the dory was while it was being towed, that is, if it indicates
relative position rather than motion. Other modifiers clear up
the ambiguity:
They quickly pulled astern the dory. (motion)
*All afternoon they pulled astern the dory. (relative
position)
All afternoon they pulled the dory astern. (relative position,
adverb moved away from verb so as not to suggest a
phrasal verb)

Although most of the phrasal-verb particles can be construed, in a resultant-condition sense, with the verb *be*, for example,

I drove them off, and they were off.

I threw it up, and it was up.

I tossed it over, and it was over.

not all of them can:

I spurred them on, *and they were on.

I urged them along, *and they were along.

This I think is a restriction on *be* rather than an indication that the particle deviates from the requirement of resultant condition. The verb *to be* requires a complement referring to a resultant *state,* that is, position (even though the combination, for example, *be off,* may be used for motion). The particles *on* and *along* refer to a condition of steady motion. Thus, whereas in *to urge forward* the particle *forward* implies movement into a forward position (and hence allows *to be forward*), *to urge on* implies movement into a condition of motion. Movement and result are given in both cases. The particle *around* shows now one and now the other:

Stop spinning around those vanes. (*They are around.)

Turn around the picture. (It is around.)

The verb *have* behaves similarly, as is to be expected in view of its affinities with *be:*

I put my shoes on. I had on my shoes.

I took out the references. I had out the references.

(But *have* is just as common in a causative sense:

I had over some friends.

I had in the neighbors to see the new baby.)

Given the two features of motion and result, one would predict that stative verbs would be found only with result and that stative verbs not compatible with it would not occur at all. This seems to be the case, as noted by Fraser (p. 20): phrasal verbs are not found with *know, hope, resemble,* and the like. In a few cases—like that of nonstative *be* just noted— a stative verb has taken on a nonstative sense:

Please hear me out.

Why don't you see off the parson and then come back? or forms part of a construction involving an embedding in which there is some other, nonstative, verb—*to get,* for example:

He wants off (in, out, up).

The adjective particles fit the hypothesis. The adjectives themselves are precisely the set that is most closely allied to verbs, with many not even requiring an affix to convert them:

He cut open the melon = He opened the melon.

I banged empty the cans = I emptied the cans.

I wrung dry the wash = I dried the wash.

A cognate object (as defined in the previous section) that fails to exhibit this verbness is predictably unacceptable:

*He shot dead the man.

*They heated red the iron.

Finally, adjectives by definition give resultant condition.

As for infinitives, the fact that they have entered the pattern confirms the notion of result since the governing verbs are causatives. If we take the three sentences

He let out the reins.

He let loose the reins.

He let go the reins.

we find that the same tree diagram, with embedded sentences equivalent to

The reins (be) out.

The reins (be) loose.

The reins go.

serves for all three:

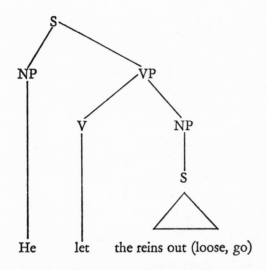

He   let   the reins out (loose, go)

I give as an example of verb-like quality the word that shows it to the highest degree: *down*. It exists as a simple verb, and many of its senses as a verb are shared with the phrasal verbs in which it appears as a particle. I follow the lettered definitions in *Webster's Third New International* which explicate the general definition "to cause to come or go down":

a. swallow: quickly downing his drink.
  He got down the pill.
  Drink it down.
  They forced me to choke it down.

b. to relegate to obscurity or forgetfulness, suppress: he could not down his regrets.
  He is trying to live down his past.

c. to get the better of, defeat: the coalition downed the bill after a lengthy fight.
  Our team spelled them down in the spelling contest.
  I faced him down and he walked off ashamed.

    d. to bring to a stop (as a game animal or an adversary) by a shot or blow: market hunters downing geese by the hundreds.

        They hunted down the poor animal.

        His Flash Gordon dream was to laser down his foes.

        He brought him down with a flying tackle.

        They shot down the observation plane.

        He flagged down the train.

        She waved down the police car.

    e. (1) to put (the helm) down.

        (2) to lower (as a signal or sail).

           They hauled down the sail.

        (3) to decrease the rate of speed of (the revolutions of a propeller).

           Slow down the propeller.

           Switch down the speed a couple of revolutions.

    f. to lay aside, put down: he downed his ax and sat on a stump to rest.

        He laid down his ax.

        I threw down the tools.

It seems, however, that the senses of *down* as a verb are specialized from its senses as a particle rather than the other way around. If we regard the particle as a quasi-verb, we are able to assign a number of additional special meanings:

    to lower (bring something to its own base), flatten:

        Push down the leaves. (to down by pushing)

        Comb down your hair. (to down by combing)

        Burn down the house. (to down by burning)

        Squash (mash, tamp, pack, sprinkle, beat, hammer) down the clods. (to down by squashing, etc.)

    to lower (bring something to a lower position):

        Carry down the blankets. (to down by carrying)

        Roll down the log.

        Hand down the boxes on top.

to incline in a downward direction:
    Slant down the plank.
    Aim (point) down the gun.
to move toward the foot:
    Turn down the covers.
    Fold down the blanket.
to diminish, reduce in volume, size, or importance:
    Boil down the syrup. (to down by boiling)
    Whittle down the stock.
    Shave down the edges.
    Pare down the potato.
    Drain down the level of the water.
    Call down the culprit.
    Scale down your demands.
    Play down the differences.
    Shake down the contents.
to bring to earth (including *d* above), fell, demount:
    Shake down the fruit. (to down by shaking)
    Don't run down the pedestrian.
    It blew down the barn.
    Chop down the tree.
    Pull down the scaffolding
    Take down the sign.
to disassemble, reduce to smaller parts:
    Break down the compound. (to down by breaking)
    Take down the engine.[3]

3. Related to this set as a kind of figurative extension is "to make or become manageable or tractable":
    Break down these figures so that we can understand them.
    Simmer down!
Kennedy calls attention (p. 37) to the distinction between *cool off* and *cool down* when applied to a nonhuman or a human object: "One can let an engine *cool down* or *off*, but . . . a person *cools off* if he has become physically warm, but he *cools down* if mentally 'heated up' or

to secure, control:
> Glue down the paper. (to down by gluing)
> Nail down the boards.
> Fasten, batten, bolt down the lid.
> Hold down the obstreperous fellow.
> Calm down your brother.

to render free of surface foreign matter, clean, give a surface treatment to:

Vacuum down the carpets. (to down by vacuuming)
> Scrub down the floors.
> Flush down the garage.
> Rake down the grass.
> Rub down the patient.

to preserve:
> Salt down the pork. (to down by salting)

to put out of operation:
> The strike closed down the factory.
> They had to shut down their business.

to record (see Spasov, p. 30):
> Let me jot down this note.
> They took down our names.

The intransitive meanings belong to most of the same sets:
> This building is coming down.
> We jetted down.
> It tipped down.

---

aroused." Actually the human versus nonhuman distinction is probably incidental to the "manageability, tractability" meaning of *down*: one would probably say
> I'll have to wait for this engine to cool down before I can work on it.
> I'll have to wait for this engine to cool off before it will be safe to put water in the radiator.

With a human object, tractability is compatible with emotional heat, not physical.

The line running down here on the map is a river.

It shrank down.

He fell down.

Settle down, my friend.

The essential verb-like quality of the particle can be seen in how far it accounts for whatever semantic features of movement or activity the phrasal verb incorporates. There is a gradient from very little to very much—in the latter, the verb proper at times does not even signify the means of the action. The following are in the order of increasing "verbness" of the particle:

Aim the gun down. (Possible, but difficult, to conceive as "down by aiming"; rather, "aim in a downward direction")[4]

Toss me down the top package. (a little more "down by tossing," but "Toss me the package" is complete)

Chop down the tree. (fairly even balance, "down by chopping")

Live down your past. ("down it by living well or long")

Spell them down. ("down them in a spelling contest")

Scale down your demands. ("down them to a lower point on the scale")

Get down the pill. (The verb proper is an empty causative.)

There is much here that reminds us of the varied transformational relationships in such compounds as *fire escape* "escape in case of fire," *mad money* "money for when you are mad," *body blow* "blow to the body," *hammer blow* "blow like a hammer's," *gunstock blow* "blow with a gunstock," and so on. But the constant is the greater or lesser verbness of the particle.

---

4. This difficulty is confirmed by that of *?Aim down the gun* as against *Toss down the package.*

CHAPTER 8

Aspect

After something is bleached white it is white, and after a person gets away, he is away. The notion of resultant condition is essential to phrasal verbs. Yet after something is fixed up it is not up, and after it has been brought about it is not about. Not all phrasal verbs embody something quite so explicit as outright resultant condition.

Kennedy (pp. 27–28) calls attention to the general use of *up* and *down* with the meaning "perfectivity," citing examples like

He chopped the tree.

He chopped down the tree.

in which the phrasal verb pictures the action as leading to a conclusion. The same example can be cited, of course, for resultant condition: resultant condition implies perfectivity. It simply appears that some of the particles—most especially *up*—have in some cases traded their full resultative meanings for the bare meaning of "result achieved." With *up*, this is quite explicit after the verb *be:*

His term is up. (finished)

The time is up.

To say *He wrote up his report* is like saying *He wrote-finished his report.* As might be expected, the less literal the particle the less likely it is to appear in predicate adjunct position:

He wrote off his losses.

?He wrote his losses off.

They ground up the lime.

?They ground the lime up.

He's holding down two jobs.

?He's holding two jobs down.

He whittled down the stick. He whittled the stick down.
(The questioned examples are normal in certain contexts; the only object in citing them is to show a tendency for terminal position to be reserved to predicate adjuncts.)

One can illustrate perfectivity by selecting contexts in which it is not appropriate:

He bowed and then left.
*He bowed down and then left.
He bowed down and wept.
He filled the ballon.
?He filled up the balloon.
He filled (filled up) the barrel.
Who's going to fill up the balloons?

Filling a balloon is not easily perfective because one can always add a bit more. Filling up a number of balloons is normal because what is accomplished is not the filling of any one but the completion of the series.

A sample of aspectual meanings. Although the notion of perfectivity can be extended to cover the bulk of phrasal verbs whose meanings have deviated from the more or less literal sum of the parts, a more explicit treatment is needed for individual particles. The question is inseparable from that of phrasal verbs as a means of lexical enrichment. What happens when particles are added to simple verbs, and how free are we to add them?[1] Fairclough (p. 73), Live (p. 436), and others have noted the general aspectual cast of phrasal verbs. Live is rightly cautious, calling the features "quasi-aspectual" and pointing out that they are not consistently matched with particular particles. Thus one could say that *turn out, grind out,* and *spin out* tend to be iterative, while *write out, print*

---

1. I do not treat other matters of conversion. Kennedy (pp. 26–27) can be consulted for transitive from intransitive and vice versa, middle from active, and so on.

out, work out, and *put out* are perfective. I believe it is possible to be a little bolder and claim that there is no real borderline between nonaspectual and aspectual uses of the particles, but rather a gradient. If a noun is described as in a condition resulting from an action, the nature of the condition will impute some kind of aspect to the action.

For the record, the term *aspect* should probably be replaced by *Aktionsart,* to reserve *aspect* for deeper and more systematic phenomena such as the progressive and the perfect tenses. But *aspect* is less awkward and will be retained here.

The following is intended only as a sample over a broad semantic range. I have chosen particles as unlike one another as possible, from the complex *up* to the univocal nautical adverbs. A serious study of the meanings of the particles and their combinations would be a book in itself.[2] In the examples, intransitives are listed before transitives and literal meanings before figurative.

Up. The primitive directional meaning was probably modified to the aspectual one by the direction that most physical acts of completion take. When a glass is filled, the level moves up toward the eye of the viewer; when a flow is suddenly checked, the level rises. This associates *up* with completion and with arrest, and also with the notion of closing a gap between the eye of the viewer and the thing viewed, which colors *up* in contrast with *down* in the following:

He came up (to me) and said . . .

She walked up (to the door) and knocked.

By hurrying we were able to catch up.

Pull up a chair and join the game.

He came down and said . . . would virtually require that there be an actual downward motion; with *up* the meaning

2. There are valuable hints in Kennedy, pp. 19–25, 27–28, 33–34.

is the perfective one of closing in on a goal.[3] In the following I indicate (1) the primitive directional meaning, literal or metaphorical; (2) extended directional meaning (something "up" is visible, for example); (3) perfective meaning as manifested in resultant condition; (4) perfective in the sense of completion or inception; and (5) perfective in the sense of attaining a high intensity:

INTRANSITIVE

(1) The work piled up.

It holds up under stress.

Let's trade up (our car for a higher-priced one).

Don't flare up at the slightest provocation. (Compare "simmer down".)[4]

(2) Ante up!

Has he turned up yet?—Yes, he showed up an hour ago.

He grew up.

(3) It shriveled up (and was left in a shriveled-up condition).

The ice broke up.

Vermont simply freezes up in winter.

(4) He clammed up.

She choked up and started to cry.

We can't just give up.

The rain let up.

---

3. *Down* may, however, refer not necessarily to downward motion but to widening a gap: *Did he walk up to the house?—No, he walked down to the road.* If we reverse this, *Did he walk down to the house?—No, he walked up to the road,* any other sense than the literally directional would be unusual.

4. The figurative meaning of the particle is not to be confused with the figurative extension or stereotyping of the phrasal verb as a whole. The *up* of *to make up a bed* was the same as that of *to make up one's mind*, though the latter has acquired its own now quite opaque sense of "decide." Similarly with the stereotyping of *to call up* to refer just to telephone calls.

We picked up where we had left off.

(5) They revved up (speeded up, hurried up). (Compare "slowed down".)[5]

TRANSITIVE

(1) He pushed up the windows.
They sent up a tray from the kitchen.
Prop it up with this.
Turn up the volume.
Chalk up the score.

(2) They brought up a different argument.
It opens up a whole new perspective.
He puffed up his cheeks.
She brought up all her children in this old farmhouse.
Put up your money.

(3) They marked up the windows.
She scratched up his face.
You've dirtied up all the glassware.
As soon as you've blackened up their faces we're ready.
They closed up the house.
He laced up his shoes.
She baked up a batch of cookies.
They paged up the materials.
They feathered up the arrows.[6]

(4) They rounded up the cattle.
He followed up the lead I gave him.
She took up dancing.

(5) Let's brighten up the colors. (Compare "tone down".)
Speed up the engine.

It is difficult if not impossible to make any clear separation

---

5. *They slowed up* is more abrupt than *They slowed down*. We would be unlikely to use **They gradually slowed up*.

6. The verbs in this set can occur without *up,* with no loss except that of the emphasis on resultant condition.

of these meanings. *To grow up* is directional, but also perfective. *To give up* is perfective but there still remains enough of the primitive sense to make synonymous verbs with incompatible senses difficult to use with *up:*

> He gave (surrendered, yielded, offered) up the property and goods.
>
> *He abandoned up the property and goods.

To abandon is to walk away from. In

> They banked up the money.
>
> *They withdrew up the money.

we detect a piling up, a perfectivity, and a residual marking in *bank up,* any one of which is inappropriate to *withdraw.* Furthermore, one can easily indulge in aspect-splitting (and get nowhere). It is possible to read in a separate inceptive aspect, but this can be interpreted as a form of perfectivity, "to make an end of a beginning":

> We picked up where we left off yesterday.
>
> He took up golf.

Related to inceptiveness is "to cause to appear, to improvise":

> She cooked up (made up, dreamed up) an excuse.
>
> She scared up a meal.

Up is the particle with virtually unlimited freedom to attach, roughly comparable to that of the prefix *re-.* If one were to hear

> Let's barter up.

the tendency would be not to react to it as deviant but as something unknown. It will be felt as deviant only if the verb proper does not admit of any relevant directional or aspectual meaning:

> *He disgusted up his friends.

Nonce-formations are normal:

> Can you give me a hand with this Chevvy?—In a minute.
>
> I've got to tire up this Rambler first.

Are they ready to do the horror scene?—No, I haven't
frightened them up enough yet.

The literal meaning is likely to be assumed with any verb
of motion. If a new verb *to helix* "to move so as to describe
a helix" were coined tomorrow, we would have

He helixed up.

immediately. Similarly an aspectual meaning will be assumed
with other verbs. Coin a verb *to friggle,* "to shred, pour na-
palm on, and ignite, as 'to friggle the records,' " and we would
soon have

They locked out the board members and friggled up the
books.

The fact that some of the verbs cited would have radically
different meanings or no meaning without the particle, for
example,

He pushed the window.

*They rounded the cattle.

is a fact of word formation and not of the semantic features
of *up.* In

They gathered the bundles.

They gathered up the bundles.

the *up* of *gathered up* is the same as the *up* of *rounded up,*
though no difference except the aspectual one can be detected
between *gather* and *gather up.* Similarly a matter of word
formation is the frequency of certain quasi-passives as against
the absence or infrequency of corresponding actives: *I'm fed
up* has no corresponding *It feeds me up,* and *He's all worked
up* (*wrought up, keyed up, wound up*) is normal while *It
works him up* is relatively unusual. Compare *I'm full up* in
which *up* combines with an adjective in a similar resultant-condition sense.

Away. In contrast with the semantic intricacy of *up, away*
displays only two, fairly compact, semantic areas. The first

centers about the literal meaning of "to (at) a distance from the scene," the second is aspectual—a kind of intensive perhaps definable by the legal phrase "without let or hindrance."

The first meaning can occur with either intransitive or transitive verbs and is extended figuratively to cover "escape, deprivation, securing from view," and the like:

INTRANSITIVE

He walked (stole, crept, flew, ambled) away.
Look away while I get dressed.
Stay away if you don't want to get into trouble.
The little boy ran away.
The thief got away.
The horse broke away.
Were you able to hide away somewhere?

TRANSITIVE

It drives away insects.
The acid ate away the exposed parts.
They sang away their blues.
He whiled away the afternoon.
Mother took away all my toys.
Put the jewels away.
They laid the gifts away until Christmas.[7]

The second meaning occurs normally only with intransitives. One can indulge in aspect chopping and distinguish iteratives and inceptives within the more general meaning of "without

7. Though pure prepositions have been excluded from this study, it is worth noting that when *with* is added to an intransitive verb of motion, the result is the same "deprivation" meaning encountered with transitives:
She walked away with my compact.
He ran away with the neighbor's wife.
He got away with her purse.
Similarly with *off*:
They drove off with my keys.
He made off with the company books.

restraint":
> The little bird sat there singing away as if its heart would burst.
> He worked away all afternoon.
> Fire away!
> They blazed away.

When the underlying meaning is transitive, the object appears regularly introduced by *at,* but sometimes by *on* or *with:*
> He keeps writing away at his books.
> *He keeps writing away his books.
> *He keeps writing his books away.
> I chopped away at the tree.
> He plugged away at his job.

This restriction makes it impossible to use *away* with verbs whose meanings do not imply an incisive effect on the object:
> *The Mayflower men moved away at our household goods all afternoon.
> *The hen kept laying away at her eggs.
> *Hazel sat blinking away at her eyes.
> *He's up there conducting away at the orchestra.
> Hazel sat blinking away.
> He's up there conducting away.

Out. This adverb is as complex as *up,* but differs in two principal ways in its aspectual meanings: it is restricted to morphology, that is, to word formation with little or no syntactic freedom, and it is mainly restricted to native, or at least to nonlearnèd, verbs. The literal "centrifugal" meaning is not so restricted. As a corollary to the lack of syntactic freedom, the aspectual meanings are more opaque. If *up* can be compared to the prefix *re-* in both its freedom to enter into new forms and its relative stability of meaning, *out* can be compared to *per-.* As an example of the antilearnèd restriction by comparison with *up,* consider:
> Can you furnish up this apartment?

Can you fit out this expedition?
*Can you equip out this expedition?
I was trying to confect up a couple of interesting puzzles.
I helped him out.
I *aided him out.
They developed up some nice reproductions.
They worked (turned) out some nice reproductions.
*They developed (evolved) out some nice reproductions.
Similarly when *excavate* and *dig* are used in the "affect" sense of "expose to view," with which *out* has its literal resultant-condition meaning, *out* is acceptable with either verb; but when the same two verbs have the "effect" sense of "create," and *out* then resembles an affix (ex-cavare = out-dig), *out* can be used only with *dig:*

> With that big machine they were able to excavate out the safe that had plunged into the basement with the fire.
> With . . . they were able to dig out . . . .
> *With a machine that size it's easy to excavate out a big hole.
> With a machine that size it's easy to dig out a big hole.

It is difficult to assemble examples to show a gradient. The following is an approximation:

INTRANSITIVE

He ambled (ventured, navigated, slunk, motored, charged) out.
I reached out for it.
The stuffing came (fell) out.
The light blew (fizzled) out.
They signed out at six o'clock.
The inside rotted (*decayed) out.
We held out for a month.
My shoes wore out.
The mine gave (played, petered) out.
It didn't work (turn, pan, *eventuate) out very well.

They lost out.

TRANSITIVE

I pushed (ran, urged, walked, persuaded) them out.

We ferreted out the facts.

They burned out the village.

Spell (write, sketch) out the conditions. (display them)

Fill out the forms

He carved (hewed, sculped, *sculptured, *fashioned) out
a statute.

I figured out the answer.

I can't make out what it is at this distance.

They found (*discovered) out the truth.

I helped him out. (to a desired outcome)

They bawled (chewed, *bellowed, *scolded) me out.

Stereotyping ranges from slight to intense:

to throw, toss, kick, heave out (get rid of)

to hand, measure, dole, send out (distribute)

to sell, work, mine out (exhaust)

The meaning "exhausted" is found in passives that may relate
to reflexives:

We've talked ourselves out. We're all talked out.

I've written myself out. I'm all written out.

or to middle voice:

My energy played out. My energy is all played out.

or to nothing, that is, no corresponding active construction:

*I tuckered out. ?It tuckered me out. I'm all tuckered out.

?I pooped out. *It pooped me out. I'm all pooped out.

Second-level metaphors (like *make up*) are extremely common:
to drop out (of school), *rub out* (a gangster), *fall out* (with
a friend), *hold out* (a promise), *mete out* (a punishment),
break out (with measles), *come out* (debut), *bring out* (a
play), *knock out* (a fighter).

On and *along*. I treat these together because of their literal and aspectual similarities, omitting the other multifarious meanings of *on* as adverb, adprep, and preposition.[8] They share the meaning of motion, of course, with the other particles, but differ from *away* and *off*, for example, in having the meanings "horizontal" and "remaining in view." Thus

The first stage dropped away (off).

The bird lifted away and was gone.

are normal, but would not be with the "horizontal" requirement of *on* and *along*. Related to the feature of "remaining in view" is the absence of counterparts with *on* or *along* for examples like:

They died off (out, away, back).

It shrank up (back, away).

—unless, of course, the action is iterative. The purely aspectual sublimation of "remaining in view" is "continuation," or durative aspect, and this we find, especially with *on*, in *keep on*, *go on* (doing something), *hold on!* (don't give up), and so forth. *On* and *along* are distinguished from each other by the features "receding" in contrast to "accompanying." In

He drove (jogged, hobbled, sailed, hurried) on.

Move on.

They drove (pushed, coaxed, spurred) him on.

one has the sensation of separation, but with

He drove along.

Move along.

They pushed him along.

we seem to be following the road with the one who is moving.

As a pair, *on* and *along* to some extent resemble *about* and *around*. Second-level metaphors and stereotypes in general are more common with *on* and *about*, whereas *along* and *around*

---

8. E.g. (*to go*) *on a trip*, (*to lecture*) *on the novel*, (*to run*) *on* (*to*) *the deck*, *to leave on* (*the lights*), *to hitch on* (*a trailer*), etc.

are more literal:

Go on! I don't believe anything like that!

Come on! You know it didn't happen that way!

Carry on.

Run along, now; I have work to do.

On is formal, serious; *along* is colloquial. To say that someone *inched on* is to imply relentless progress against heavy odds; *to inch along* may be simply playful. Similarly

They don't get on well.

They don't get along well.

How are things coming on?

How are things coming along?

are synonymous pairs, but the second member is a step lower in register. And similarly on the historical scale: *to egg on* (dating from the sixteenth century) and *to string along* "deceive" (twentieth century).

To go on followed by an infinitive combines durative and inceptive aspects: it refers to resuming an action that was in progress before and has been interrupted either by the actor himself or by the observer who stops to contemplate. It is therefore not consonant with either the grammatical perfective or the grammatical progressive:

He went on to say that he hadn't intended to hurt anyone's feelings, but . . .

In the next chapter he goes on to explain the reasons for adopting this solution.

*Has he gone on to say that it wasn't really intentional?

*If I were going on to explain the reasons . . .⁹

Forth. This is of interest as the only particle no longer pro-

9. Acceptable if iterative (for the perfect) and intentional (for the progressive):

Has he ever gone on to explain what he had in mind?

I was going on to say what I had in mind but they interrupted me.

ductive. Although it occurs in a good many combinations, they are all more or less fossilized. We would form a new phrasal verb with *out,* not with *forth,* unless to appear intentionally quaint:

Our plane jetted out over the ocean.

*Our plane jetted forth over the ocean.[10]

In some cases, for example, *to sally forth,* the verb as well as the particle has dropped from colloquial usage, and in others we find *out* but not *forth* usable with the more colloquial of two verbs:

He pulled out his sword.

*He pulled forth his sword.

He drew out his sword.

He drew forth his sword.

Lincoln's Gettysburg Address has probably helped to preserve *bring forth* (*to bring forth* a new nation but *to bring out* a play), but intransitive *set forth* has yielded to *set out, give forth* to *give out, hold forth* (a hope) to *hold out,* and so on. Among those still undiminished are

They put forth a tremendous effort.

He can hold forth on any subject.

It called forth a stern rebuke.

He set forth his views.

Set forth transitive now contrasts with *set out,* which is generally used for concrete objects:

They set out the dishes and silverware.

Astern and other "literal" adverbs. At this extreme, first-level metaphors are rare and meanings that could be viewed as aspectual are virtually absent. Second level metaphors are readily found, and some have been stereotyped, for example,

---

10. It is barely possible that *forth* might be used to suggest that the action itself is formal, e.g., in reference to a military formation: *The bombers jetted forth over the ocean.*

We turned aside the objections.

He stepped aside for his successor.

They set apart a portion of their inheritance.

Summary. Phrasal verbs present a semantic gradient from highly concrete meanings of direction and position to highly abstract meanings akin to aspects. At the first extreme an example like

He pulled the boat alongside.

tells nothing but the direction of motion and position of rest. At the second, an example like

He drew up the list.

is purely aspectual. Yet fundamentally the two extremes are akin. There is a deep-seated relationship between notions of action, state, progression, inception, completion, and the like, on the one hand and notions of direction and position on the other—a kind of geometry of semantics.

CHAPTER 9

Stereotyping

Syntax or morphology? In Chapter 3, the phrasal verb was viewed as a combination variable syntactically. Whether we said *He put off the decision* or *He put the decision off* made no difference to the identity of *put off*. We were concerned with the dynamics of the sentence as a whole, and the verb was "the same" in both cases.

We must now inquire to what extent the elements of phrasal verbs may be captured in one position or another, yielding combinations that are relatively or absolutely inseparable and thus carrying on the lexicalization of word order that long since destroyed *overstep,* for example, as a variant of *step over.* From a rule of syntax we pass to a rule, or a hodgepodge of rules, of morphology. An analogy from a more familiar area, that of noun compounds, will help to make the distinction clearer. There is a syntactic rule that allows nouns to modify nouns. One may freely refer to a *Mars orbit* or a *rocket takeoff.* But while the same rule appears to apply to *arm + pit → armpit,* we are not free to say **legpit* or **kneepit* (we have to say *the hollow of the knee*). And while *springtime, summertime,* and *wintertime* follow the rule, there is no **falltime* or **autumntime.* An automobile develops *engine trouble,* not **motor trouble,* but a company that manufactures automobiles is a *motor company* (*Ford Motor Company*), not an **engine company*—the latter would refer to a fire department. The parts in these combinations may no longer be freely assembled and disassembled. Also the meaning specializes: *scout* is not the same in *Indian scout* and *boy scout.*

The phrasal verb similarly is at the border of syntax and

morphology. There is clearly a different order of relatedness in
  Have you taken in the wash yet?
  Have you taken the wash in yet?
from that in
  She takes in washing (sewing, boarders, roomers).
  *She takes washing in.[1]
It seems that when a rule of syntax brings together particular
words more frequently than others, the high-frequency combinations tend to fossilize. (Or perhaps this puts the facts backwards. If the culture institutionalizes a thing or operation, the
elements that freely composed its name when it was viewed
as a mere passing phenomenon lose part or all of their primitive sense and primitive freedom.)

Levels of stereotyping. But phrasal verbs are special in that
they represent a kind of double layer of compounding. The
particles are, to begin with, more or less affixal in nature,
and the very fact that the combinations pass the definite-noun-
phrase test defines them as compounds of a sort. The first
compositional layer is the simple association of a verb and
a particle. The second layer is a differentiation *within* the
phrasal verb, related to the varying positions of the particle
and other factors.

The question of stereotyping at the first level is one that
we have arbitrarily cut off at a certain point by the application
of the definite-noun-phrase test. Yet below that point we find
an infinitude of concretions, of loosely connected but nevertheless to some extent ready-made combinations that give the lie
to notions of a syntax made of elementary particles that can
join at will. Consider the three synonyms *to strike down, to
declare unconstitutional,* and *to find unconstitutional.* Neither

1. This is not a rigid restriction. *Why don't you take a bit of washing
in once in a while if you need extra cash?* is normal. The effect of
added modification is discussed in Chapter 12.

of the phrases with adjectives passes the definite-noun-phrase test:

The Supreme Court struck down the law.

*The Supreme Court declared (found) unconstitutional the law.

Yet they differ in terms of a less exacting test:

The Supreme Court will find (declare) any such law as that unconstitutional.

The Supreme Court will declare unconstitutional any such law as that.

?The Supreme Court will find unconstitutional any such law as that.

—*to declare unconstitutional* is a better first-level "compound" than *to find unconstitutional*.

Second-level stereotyping has been touched on already in the chapters on verb-modification versus noun-modification (Chapter 6) and aspect (Chapter 8). There is a tendency for particles to be captured in either the post-verbal position (*to take in washing*) or the post-noun position (*to bring the victims to, to tell two things apart*), especially the the former, in some particular sense. Under aspect some consideration was given to second-level metaphors, which make up the bulk of second-level stereotypes. The overlap of these two illustrates the resourcefulness of the phrasal verb in producing "transparent" compounds which match Latinate forms—for example, *take back* as against *return*— which are "opaque" in English but were correspondingly transparent in Latin.[2]

---

2. To recapitulate: A first-level metaphor is one in which the literal meaning of the particle is extended: the literal "up" of *go up* becomes the figurative "up" of *load up*. A second-level metaphor is one in which the meaning of the phrasal verb as a whole (perhaps but not necessarily including an already metaphorized particle) is figuratively extended: one literally *makes up* a bed or *rubs out* a mistake and figuratively *makes up* a face or *rubs out* an adversary. First-level stereotyping is the simple combining

There is also what might be termed third-level stereotyping, in which the entire verb phrase is frozen. These are "idioms." They are worth exemplifying, but no more. Most have verb and particle side by side:

to put on the dog
to put on airs
to strike up an acquaintance
to strike up the band
to take up arms
to turn over a new leaf
to let off steam
to bring up the rear
to choose up sides
to shut up shop
to pluck up courage[3]

but some have the particle after the noun object:

to keep one's hand in (keep in practice)
to put one's foot down (stand in firm and authoritative opposition)
to cry one's eyes (heart) out
to talk someone's head (arm) off
to keep one's shirt on (be patient)

and a few have a choice:

That joke brought the house down.

---

of a verb proper with a particle; the meaning is as nearly additive as can be. A second-level stereotype is a phrasal verb that is no longer semantically additive. In Fairclough's terms (pp. 77–79), we find literal (my first-level stereotype), metaphorical, e.g. *Dusk was creeping up on us* (my second-level metaphor), and figurative (my second-level stereotype). He points out that literal and metaphorical involve the same lexical item (*to rub out* would be the "same" phrasal verb in both senses), while figurative (*to come across* = to find) involves a different lexical item (in this case, different from *to come across a field*). Spasov (p. 48) terms the same three classes nonidiomatic, semi-idiomatic, and idiomatic.

3. Fraser, p. 68.

That joke brought down the house.

Other forms of fossilizing will not be treated here—for example the restriction to the passive of *left over* and *put out* "annoyed," but not *held over* nor *kept over*.[4] "Stereotyping" in the remainder of the discussion refers to second-level stereotypes.

Evidence for stereotyping. The intuitive evidence is of course semantic, and it is reflected in the definitions that are required in a dictionary. No definition of *to shape* or definition of *up*, either literal or aspectual, will account for the meaning of *shape up* in

If he doesn't shape up I'm going to fire him.

But there is also more objective evidence in three areas: phonology, lapses, and ordering relative to other elements.

The phonological evidence is in the reduction, especially vowel reduction, to be found in highly frequent stereotypes. A number of these have dialectal or eye-dialectal spellings: *gwan!* for go on!, *giddap!* for *get up* (addressed to a horse), *g'way!* for *go away!* The *let down* of *What did they let down?* is not phonetically reduced, but *sit down* is normally pronounced [sɪɾawn] with alveolar flap.

Lapses in which affixes are wrongly placed are more apt to occur with tightly bound units. Examples from another area are *mother-in-laws, three bourbon and sodas.* I have heard the following:

Go overing the exercises . . .

Are we set asiding the rule?

There are at least two accepted forms that have resulted from this process: *to doff* and *to don,* historically *to do off* and *to do on.* The earlier and later past tense forms are illustrated in

4. These are treated by Fairclough, p. 53.

He did off his cloak. (*Or,* He off did his cloak.)

He doffed his cloak.

and of course the *-ing* forms are respectively *doing off* and *doffing.* (A similar contemporary form is noted by Maher: *shunpiking* "shunning turnpikes." This is possibly denominal, however, based on the noun *shunpike,* a road other than a "pike" or freeway.) Though it is not a lapse except from the puristic standpoint, the form in which agent nouns began to multiply in the 1920's and 1930's evidences an unwillingness to take just the verb proper as the carrier of the *-er* suffix. The classical form is of course exemplified by *runner-up,* but popular coinages preferred the type *builder-upper, loser-outer.* Spasov cites *tearer-downer* (p. 40).

The syntactic evidence is of two types, both involving displacement of the particle. The first was suggested by Palmer (p. 186); it notes the unacceptability of the particle in initial position. There is no second-level stereotyping in

Down they sat.

Away he flew.

On they came.

but there is in the phrasal verbs of

He broke down. *Down he broke.

He gave up. *Up he gave.

They found out. *Out they found.[5]

Palmer's test determines fairly well whether a particle has lost its literal meaning but fails to detect stereotypes in which the

5. Palmer's test is better than he thought. He regarded *Out he looked* as unacceptable not only when used in response to *Look out!* but also in a literal sense and concluded that there must be instances of literal uses of the particle that resist displacement as much as transferred ones. This may be true of some verbs, but not of *look out,* as witness

    I told him to put his head out of the window and look around—so out he looked, the damned fool, and nearly got his head knocked off for his pains.

literal meaning is retained but the phrasal verb is specialized in some other way. We would probably regard *to set out* (on a journey) and *to set off* (on a journey) as equally stereotyped, yet the examples.

So off they set on one of the longest journeys in history.

*So out they set on one of the longest journeys in history. suggest that *off* has kept more of its literal directional meaning. This is confirmed by a question that might be asked relevant to this statement:

Are they off yet?

*Are they out yet?[6]

The second kind of displacement is by interpolating an adverb so as to separate the particle from the verb (Test 6, Chapter 1). With intransitives, this can be done directly. If we were to list the following phrasal verbs, *to clatter on, to purr away, to catch on* (understand), *to march in, to fall in* (form ranks), *to soar off, to take off* (depart), *to dart up, to grow up* (reach maturity), and *to break off* (to be interrupted), we would sense that the ones I have defined are the ones that need a special definition; and we find that they are the ones that resist separation:

They clattered noisily on.

The cat sat there, purring contentedly away.

*He caught quickly on.

The troops marched briskly in.

*The troops fell briskly in.

The plane soared thunderously off.

*The plane took thunderously off.

6. The transferred sense of *out* is "in the field," as can be seen in
He's off on a survey for the Ford Foundation.
He's out on a survey for the Ford Foundation.
They're off shopping somewhere.
They're out shopping.

The rabbit darted quickly up.

*A child grows quickly up.

The limb broke completely off.

?The negotiations broke completely off.[7]

(There is no problem if the adverb is not interpolated:

A child quickly grows up.

A child grows up quickly.)

One often finds a deverbal noun with precisely such a stereo-typed verb as its origin—*takeoff*, for example. Compare also *letdown, backdown, walkout,* and *holdup* with the following:

He climbed into the bosun's chair and they let him gently down.

*At the last moment they let him gently down in spite of their previous promises to help. ("They gently let him down" is acceptable.)

The road was blocked, there was no going ahead, so he backed timidly down the way he had come.

*He had given us his word, but at the last moment he backed timidly down.

The workmen walked angrily out on no pretext at all.

*The workmen walked angrily out on strike.

I handed him the blazing stick and he held it calmly up.

*The thief stopped us and held us calmly up.

It seems that the moment stereotyping occurs, no matter how vivid the metaphor that remains, the resistance to interpolation sets in:

He pulled the pieces loose and tossed them nonchalantly off.

*He memorized his jokes and tossed them nonchalantly off.

---

7. Some intensive adverbs can be interpolated (see pp. 134–137):

The troops fell right in.

The child has grown straight up.

The negotiations broke clean off.

The weight slid to one side of the cockpit and dropped abruptly out.

*He knew he was going to fail, so he dropped abruptly out.

(Again, *dropout*.) As these last examples suggest, with transitive verbs the test is best applied with the noun object out of the way. It can be with a pronoun, as in some of the foregoing, or with a subordinate clause:

This is (these are) . . .

the money he gave happily away.

*the subject he brought angrily up.

the problem he thought steadily through.

*the information he handed gladly over.

?the suggestion he turned abruptly aside.

*the suggestion he put abruptly off.

the facts they ferreted quickly out.

*the forms they filled quickly out.

A stereotype may reach up to third level and incorporate idiomatically one adverb where another—even synonymous—one may be doubtful:

They pressed bravely (resolutely, determinedly, courageously, doughtily) on.

They carried bravely on.

*They carried determinedly on.

Kinds of stereotypes. The extreme case is the one that permits no shift of the particle. Examples with *let* are frequent:

He put up a good fight (a show of resistance, a good argument). *He put a good fight up.

This carries off the prize. *This carries the prize off.

They found out the truth. *They found the truth out.

He let out a yell. *He let a yell out.

He let fly (with) a string of oaths. *He let a string of oaths fly.

He let fall a couple of snide remarks. *He let a couple of snide remarks fall.

Yours are bad enough, leave (let) alone the others. * . . . leave (let) the others alone.

Let go (of) my leg! *Let my leg go! (Let go of me. Let me go.)

(Not all the restrictions here are absolute; see pp. 164–165.) The bifurcation that has occurred with *let go* is a typical effect of the literalness of a terminal particle[8] and of the physical reassortment of the constituents. Both senses can be defined as "to release," but in *let go* (*of*) *the man* the meaning is "unhand him," whereas in *Let the man go* it refers to removing constraint of any kind. In the latter the position of *man* still allows taking it as both the object of *let* and the subject of *go*—there is, in other words, an embedded sentence. In the former this has been lost. But there are phrasal verbs grammatically identical to *let go* that are not restricted in this way:

He let slip the opportunity.

He let the opportunity slip.

Cases like these should be distinguished from apparently similar ones which are not restricted as stereotypes but by a grammatical rule that prohibits moving the particle over a sentential object:

Don't let on who you are.

*Don't let who you are on.

They found out who he was.

*They found who he was out.

There are varying degrees even here: *to let on* will not permit any separation; *to let out, to find out, to bring up,* and the

---

8. Literalness is relative. It does not necessarily refer to the directional-positional meaning of a particle but to any meaning that is more or less proper to it. *He put up the money* differs from *He put the money up* in that the latter signifies more clearly a resultant condition.

like, do permit insertion of a nonsentential object or a pronoun:

> You won't let on you know who I am, will you?—*No, I won't let it on. ("I won't let on," "I won't let on anything like that" are acceptable.)
>
> You won't let (it) out that you know who I am, will you?—No, I won't let it out.[9]

The most frequent case is that of a particle captured next to the verb in a second-level stereotype that is only slightly specialized from the literal meaning. Both positions of the particle are still possible, but the stereotyped meaning is relatively more frequent when the particle is next to the verb and the nonstereotyped meaning when the two are separated:

> He wouldn't take back the ring so she kept on wearing it.
>
> He took the ring back and demanded his money.
>
> Why did the manager let off this employee? He had no right to fire him!
>
> Why did the manager let this employee off? Today's no holiday, he has a job to do.
>
> I'm going to do over this dress and see if I can't make it look more in style.
>
> I'm going to do this dress over; I didn't get it right the first time.
>
> They cut short the conversation.
>
> They cut the stick short.

A figure of speech may be quite vividly related to the literal meaning, and still lead to a closer link with the verb:

> They covered the bodies up.
>
> They covered up (concealed) the crime.

9. *Let* and *leave* are also involved in stereotypes that are not phrasal verbs:
Let the man be! *Let be the man!
Leave the man alone! *Leave alone the man!

They threw the yoke off (the ox).

They threw off (liberated themselves from) the yoke.

He threw the ball up.

He threw up (vomited) his breakfast.

They threw the man out.

They threw out (discarded) the odd quantities.

My partner just brought some guy ín. I think it's a friend of his.

My partner just brought ín (arrested) some guy. I think he caught him trying to break in a jewelry store.[10]

The stereotyping dovetails so neatly at times with the normal effects of the prosody that one is hard put to decide whether to describe it in terms of one or the other. In the example with *do over* one can think of a stereotype meaning "remodel," but it makes just as much sense to explain the difference in meaning as due to the semantic focus on *dress:* in *do over the dress* the dress as an entity is in question—it is the center of concern, and its very nature may be changed; but in *do the dress over* the dress is (more or less) presupposed and the focus is the repeated action. In the example with *let off* we can think of a stereotype meaning "dismiss," but *let off an employee* focuses on employee—the status of the person as employee is in question; in *let an employee off* the employee is presupposed and the action of releasing is the center of concern. In *cut short* we can think of a stereotype meaning "interrupt"; but *cut short a conversation* focuses on there being or not being a conversation, whereas *cut a conversation short* takes there being a conversation for granted but is concerned with its length. The uncertainty here should not be surprising if we realize that new linguistic units come regularly from the womb of old grammatical processes.

10. L. A. Hill, p. 90, lists the synonymous and more thoroughly stereo-typed *run in* "arrest."

Among the cases of relatively slight specialization it is possible to find rather numerous examples with two senses—differentiated more or less by position—both of which are found in a single synonymous simple verb. Thus *to let off* X and *to let* X *off* are both represented in the two senses of the simple verb *release* ("to fire" and "to excuse"). Similarly for *find out* = *discover* and *talk over* = *discuss:*

They found out the assassin. (discovered his identity)

They found the assassin out. (discovered him to the world, exposed him)

Let's get together and talk over things—like when we used to play together and things like that.

Let's get together and talk things over—we ought to be able to find a way to an understanding.

They talked over their problems. (considered them)

They talked their problems over. (dealt with them verbally)

At the other extreme we find adverbs that are so clearly predicative adjuncts that they cannot stand next to the verb. This being the case, the combination is by definition not a phrasal verb; yet their defectiveness seems not to be inherent, but rather due to a kind of conflict-of-homonyms polarization. The existence of a firm second-level stereotype on the one hand, and a vividly directional-positional particle on the other, excludes the latter from joining the verb. There is also some connection, apparently, with the vividness of the metaphor. Thus *to heave up* has its literal meaning and also the vividly metaphorical meaning "to vomit," yet both meanings admit both positions; similarly with *to throw out* "to bounce":

He heaved up his breakfast.

He heaved his breakfast up.

They heaved up the load of coal.

They heaved the load of coal up.

They threw out the garbage.

They threw the garbage out.

They threw out the man.

They threw the man out.

But this is not true of *leave out* "omit," *put out* "extinguish," *hold together* "bind," *hold apart* "keep separate," or *keep up* "maintain," as against the same verbs when the particle retains its literal reading (as shown by the more general, but still not exclusive freedom to combine with *to be*):

You've left out the clothes—your list is not complete.

You've left the clothes out—your list is not complete.

You've left the clothes out and they're all wet from the rain. (The clothes *are out*.)

*You've left out the clothes and they're all wet from the rain.

They put out the lights.

They put the lights out.

They put the man out. (He *is out*, literally.)

*They put out the man.[11]

It holds together (apart) the halves.

It holds the halves together (apart).

The referee held the opponents together (apart).

*The referee held together (apart) the opponents. (Contrast "The referee brought together the opponents.")[12]

She keeps up her membership.

11. The examples with *put* show gradience in two respects. First, *to put out lights* yields *The lights are out*. *Out* has developed a "proper" sense (unlike *The clothes are out* applied to omission from a list, but like *That's out!* applied to forced omission from consideration) which is readily construed with *be* and nevertheless is a shade less literal than *to put someone out*. Second, the prosody intervenes in that while *They put out the man* is unlikely, *They put out the troublemakers* is acceptable—the news value of the latter noun justifies end position.

12. Again, in both senses—as with *out* in the preceding footnote—both things *are together* (*apart*), even in the fastening sense, though in addition they are stuck together. Since *to be* can be used with these particles, it is not as reliable as Fairclough thought it to be (p. 81) as a test for there being no particle polarity: *to be together* and *to be apart* are normal and so are *to hold together* and *to hold apart*—*together* and *apart* are polar opposites.

She keeps her membership up.

She keeps people up till all hours. (They *are up*.)

*She keeps up people till all hours.

The notion of homonymic conflict is supported by the unpredictableness already noted, which is typical in these cases, and also by the sensitivity to context—there are instances in which the avoidance does not occur unless the context produces a conflict. So for *tell off* in the two senses of "score," the first "to tally" and the second "to upbraid":

The clerk told off the numbers as the members filed by.

The clerk told the numbers off as the members filed by.

The clerk told off the members as they filed by.

*The clerk told the members off as they filed by.

It is difficult not to take the last example in the "upbraid" sense, given the human object.[13]

A more obvious instance of homonymic conflict, involving a collision of transitivity as well as lexical meaning, is that of the two uses of *get off*:

The lawyer got the prisoner off.

The lawyer got off the prisoner.

Since other similar cases give no problem, for example,

We got the report in.

We got in the report.

can both be taken in the same sense, the absolute polarity of *get off* must be due to the comparatively greater incongruity of one of the meanings. It is not because *off* in this sense is restricted to end position, because

---

13. Though in this example it is not exactly true that there is a *be* paraphrase for the resultant condition, that is, we could not say *They are off*, nevertheless there is an element of literalness that is absent in the "tally" sense: *off* is also to be found in the synonymous expression *He told them where to get off*, and in other vaguely associated expressions having to do with "riddance" of something undesirable: *bump off, let off* (with a reprimand), *kiss off*.

The judge let off the prisoner with a light sentence.
is normal.

Other restrictions on stereotypes. As with the effect of the prosody in *do over* and *let off*, it is difficult to decide sometimes whether an apparent stereotype reflects in some way the operation of a rule of grammar. We can be fairly sure that no rule determines the fact that *to hand down* "transmit" and *to hang up* "fixate" normally appear only in the passive voice:

These traits are handed down from father to son.

He got hung up on the black power thing.

But what of the position of the particle in a phrasal verb such as *to make up* "constitute"? When we compare

The fifty states that make up the nation.

*The nation that the fifty states make up.

*The fifty states that make the United States up.

These are the points that sum up my position.

?This is the position that the points sum up.

?These are the points that sum my position up.

These are the points that round out my position.

?This is the position that the points round out.

?These are the points that round my position out.
with

The states that are this nation.

*The nation that these states are.

it appears that there is some restriction on end position of copulative or copula-like verbs with a fronted predicate noun, which prevents placing the particle at the end. But this in turn can be laid to the prosody. Copulas are normally "empty" verbs.[14] They accordingly are not given the position of semantic focus. If the status of mere copula is abrogated, the verb (in

14. This is not always true. Compare the pure identity use in *You shouldn't doubt that he is John.—*John he is; I don't deny it; but* . . . with the descriptive *You shouldn't doubt that he is a man.—A man he is;*

this case specifically *make up*) can go at the end:

The states that constitute this nation.

The states by (of) which this nation is constituted.

The states that form this nation.

The nation that these states form.

Why do they insist on that insane roll call at every convention? What importance do all those names have?—

You've got to remember that they're the states that make our country úp!

In other senses of *make up* there is no problem:

She makes up the beds. She makes the beds up.

The rule against moving a particle over a sentential object has already been mentioned (pp. 120–121). Yet this again is not absolute. It depends in part on the kind of sentential object, in part on the literalness of the particle, and in part on the prosody.

On the first score, there is a small set of phrasal verbs that appear to function as quasi-progressive-auxiliaries, and reveal a state of affairs in the *-ing* forms perhaps allied to the action nominal contrast (Test 3, pp. 8–10): a difference between an *-ing* that is part of the verbal and a closely allied nominalized *-ing* that is not. There are a number of phrasal verbs that refer to not doing something. They are all freely used with the nominalized *-ing:*

They put off their studying. (their study)

They put their studying off.

He gave up his smoking. (his habit)

I don't deny it; but . . . This appears to relate to the phenomenon of degree words, since it applies to degree versus nondegree adjectives as well as nouns: *This chart is astronomical.—*Astronomical it is, but* . . . ,* in which *astronomical* is a nondegree identifying adjective, differs from *These budget figures are astronomical.—Astronomical they are, but* . . . It is as if the copula joined to a descriptive (degree) adjective were a true verb.

He gave his smoking up.

He held off his complaining. (his complaints)

He held his complaining off.

But when the -ing is part of the verbal, only one position is normal; to the same set of verbs we can now add *leave off*:

They put off studying. *They put studying off.

He gave up smoking. *He gave smoking up.

He held off complaining. *He held complaining off.

He left off complaining. *He left complaining off.

These, like their companion simple verbs, resemble auxiliaries: *They postponed deciding* means "They did not decide for the time being"; *They postponed their deciding* (*their decision*) does not have this resemblance to the verbal *did* (*not*) *decide*. Similarly, *He stopped grumbling* and *He stopped his grumbling*.

Where the sentential object is an infinitive, the only examples I have are *let on* and *make out,* which are inseparable:

Don't let on to understand. *Don't let to understand on.

He made out to believe me. *He made to believe me out.

Where the sentential object is a clause introduced by a *wh-*word (who, where, which, how, and the like), there is more freedom, and the prosody along with the literalness of the particle has a deeper effect. A particle that has little meaning of its own is unlikely to get the semantic focus of terminal position. The following will hardly allow separation of verb and particle:

He told off what he had found, piece by piece.

*He told what he had found off, piece by piece.

I found out how they had done it.

*I found how they had done it out.

I can't make out who it is.

*I can't make who it is out.

But other particles are less inhibited:

That Congressman always pushes what he wants through.

Regretfully, he gave what he had found back.

What clauses can have concrete referents and are more likely to make the separation than other clauses—the phrasal verb, and consequently the particle, tends to have a literal value, which is not true with "discourse" and "knowing" verbs. In case of an ambiguity, concreteness will be attributed to the article in final position:

The fool gave away what he had.

The fool gave what he had away.

It brings back what we used to have.

It brings what we used to have back.

The first *give away* can mean either "betray" or "donate" and the first *bring back* can be either "be reminiscent of" or "restore"; but the second members of the pairs are practically limited to "donate" and "restore," with the literal meanings of *away* and *back*. By the same token, an ambiguity may rule out a particle in final position:

They talked what had happened over.

*They talked what he had done over.

The problem of sentential elements *within* objects, for example,

He brought back the things we lost.

He brought the things back that we lost.

He brought the things we lost back.

is more complex and is saved for the next chapter.

Extended stereotypes. There are numerous stereotypes that are more or less idiomatic (that is, semantically nonadditive) involving a phrasal verb and a preposition. Such combinations are not different in kind from those already noted composed of simple verbs and prepositions, for example, *cope with, rely on, carp at, see to, bear with, do with* (I could do with a glass of cold water right now) and the like, which have not been included in this study, and are accordingly given only token recognition here. Compare *do away with* and *dispense with, get along without* and *do without.*

There is sometimes the question whether a phrasal verb is actually involved, or rather some special compound preposition. Thus in

I leave the decision to you.

I leave the decision up to you.

The decision is *up to* you.

it is not clear whether a phrasal verb *leave up* should be recognized. We cannot say

*I leave up the decision to you.

But the perfective meaning of *up* is clearly present: the speaker washes his hands of the matter.

The transparency of the idiom varies. We have already noted examples with *away* (Chapter 9, note 8). In

He ran away with her purse.

He escaped with her purse.

run away with is transparent, but still is closer to "steal" than *escape with* would be. (There seems to be a kind of semantic blend with *Away with her purse!*) Similarly in

He made off with the money.

He absconded with the money.

But

He got away with her purse.

He got away with murder.

shows a step in the direction of opaqueness. *To put up with* is completely opaque.

In some extensions we find exactly the same kind of semantic bifurcation that was noted above in relation to the change of position of the particle in *find out* and *talk over.* Thus *to make good* covers two senses of *to fulfil,* "to replenish" and "to keep":

He made good the losses. He made them good.

He made good on his word. He made good on it.[15]

Again as with simple verbs, there are combinations with *it*. The *it* sometimes has a more or less defined antecedent:

Can we make the next signal?—We can make it if you hurry.

The poor guy wanted to get back to his home town but he never made it.

He promised to make up the loss to me but he never did make it up.

I'm sorry to have hurt him; I hope to make it up to him some day.

Why do you have to take your displeasure out on your wife?—I have to take it out on somebody.

It's all right for you to be sore but don't take it out on me.

At other times there is no antecedent:

He lords it over his brother.

They're roughing it up in Alaska somewhere.

He has it in for me.

I've been living it up in Paris.

If you want to mix it up with your brother do it somewhere else than in the living room.

You two don't hit it off very well, do you?

Summary. One can fairly make two generalizations about stereotyping in phrasal verbs: it is infinitely graded, and it reacts intricately with prosodic contrasts and contrasts due to verb versus noun modification. Kennedy was right when he declared (p. 8) that "it would be a hopeless undertaking to classify every verb-adverb combination as either close enough to be termed a verb-adverb compound, or loose enough to be called merely an adverbial modification."

15. All the same, the two are close enough to interchange when the prosody makes it necessary.

CHAPTER 10

More Than One Particle

Two particles combined are commonplace, and more than two can be heard occasionally:
We hurried on through.
They sailed along by.
The cat crawled back in under.
Come on back up over!
I tried to push báck dówn ín the catchbolt.
Multiple particles may or may not pass the definite-noun-phrase test. There is much more gradience here than with single particles:
He took back in the copies.
Bring on over the newcomer.
They pushed on the plan. They pushed through the plan.
　*They pushed on through the plan.
He pulled back the curtains. He pulled aside the curtains.
　?He pulled back aside the curtains.
Bring back Joe. Bring in Joe. *Bring back in Joe.
The news value of the noun needs to be relatively high.
　Combinations with particular particles. The sequence of particles requires a study in itself. There seems to be a ranking whereby the last particle is most resultant-condition-like, while preceding ones are more direction-like or more aspect-like:
It slipped down off.
?It slipped off down.
On and *along,* but especially *on,* referring to a continuation rather than a position, may occur before any of the particles referring to a position, as if to intensify the motion-through feature of the following particle:
They dragged along across their wounded.

*They dragged across along their wounded.

He hurried up through. He hurried up on through.

Some rather involved permutations are theoretically possible:

Come back up through on over.

Come back on up through over.

Come on back up through over.

Along could replace *on,* but is unlikely except in the last example:

Come along back up through over.

Since **on on* is avoided, *along* can replace the first *on:*

Come along on.

Similarly, in all likelihood, **on off,* because of the apparent incongruity, hence

Come along off.

Similarly, *back* for "repetition" or "return" is unlikely to occur at the end of a series of particles:

Come on back in.

Come back on in.

*Come in on back.

*Come on in back.[1]

Adjectives, giving more naturally the terminal result, come last:

I pried up loose the lid.

*I pried loose up the lid.

He planed the board down smooth.

*He planed the board smooth down.

If there is clearly a natural order of positions through which the motion takes place, the particles arrange themselves

1. Fraser correctly observes (p. 91) that combinations of particles are most apt to be found in imperative sentences. It seems that giving instructions as to sequences of actions makes the imperative the most natural setting for such combinations. The following, observed on a shoe-shine machine at Newcastle-on-Tyne, would be unacceptable in a different construction: "1. Insert coinage. 2. *Press toe cap upward in.*"

accordingly:

Crawl down in.

Walk up over.

It is unlikely that two particles both signifying result will occur together:[2]

*They broke the door down out.

*We cut the lines away off.

This is perhaps the reason why the aspectual *up* is not followed by a particle signifying result:

*He chopped up off the limb.

*I tried to cut up open the melon.

*They burned the leaves up away.

(Directional *up* is another matter:

We raked the leaves up out.

And so are adjectives which would not in this connection qualify as particles themselves:

She stirred the mixture up smooth. She stirred up the mixture smooth.

She chopped the nuts up fine. She chopped up the nuts fine.

He wadded the paper up loose. He wadded up the paper loose.

—contrast the genuine adjective-particle use of *open:*

He pushed back open the door. *He pushed back the door open.)

Intensifiers. Not many combinations with adjectives pass the definite-noun-phrase test (except for *open* and *loose,* as usual), but in any position it is obvious that the adjective follows the adverb. In the following I use verb-adjective combinations which are the semantically cognate object type found earlier

2. This does not refer to the particle as straight adverb. An example like *Chop the limb off down!* uses *down* as the equivalent of *downward,* not in the sense of a resultant condition. See p. 87.

to pass the definite-noun-phrase test:

?I wrung out dry the wash. I wrung the wash out dry. *I wrung the wash dry out.

?She polished up bright the brasswork. She polished the brasswork up bright. *She polished the brasswork bright up.

?She boiled down thick the syrup. She boiled the syrup down thick. *She boiled the syrup thick down.

?I banged out empty the cans. I banged the cans out empty. *I banged the cans empty out.

Yet there is a curious reversal. To lay a basis for it, we notice first that certain adverbs can be used as intensive modifiers of particles (adverb or adjective), whether or not the combination passes the definite-noun-phrase test:

The adult programmes carry straight on from the children's hour.[3]

When he stopped he went flat out.[4]

Go straight back.[5]

They cleaned it all up.[6]

Come right along.

It blew the handles right off.[7]

It left quite open the question.

It makes quite plain what he has in mind.

3. Fairclough, p. 48.
4. Spasov, p. 56. He calls these qualifiers "definers."
5. L. A. Hill, p. xxi.
6. Fraser, p. 38.
7. *Right* is such a common qualifier that it has become virtually fused in some combinations. Thus *right out*, as L. A. Hill notes (p. 140), means "without concealment":

He came out with it. (He was frank about it.)
*He came out and told me.
He came right out and told me.
*We laughed out.
We laughed right out.

It gives dead away your intentions.

He pushed the helm hard aport.

A few adjectives—of the semantically cognate object type, apparently—have wedged themselves into this pattern and can precede an adverbial particle as an intensive modifier; in fact it is hard to say, considering such items as *straight* and *dead* from the previous set of examples, when we are dealing with adjectives and when with adverbs:

He stood the pole straight up. (Compare "He stood the pole up straight.")

It blew the handles clean off. (It blew the handles off clean.)

They brushed the lint clear away. (They brushed the lint away clear.)

Keep your head high up. (Keep your head up high.) [8]

He screwed the bolts tight up. (He screwed the bolts up tight.)

Tight up is apparently a stereotype, as we do not find

*They battened the covers tight down.

and it makes one think of a possible echoic phenomenon: *flat, straight, quite, right, tight.* The recent popular adjectivization of *uptight* supports the notion of stereotypes here, as do the standard *right away, straightaway,* and *right off.* This must be related to the phenomenon of degree adverbs in general:

He took it completely off. He took it off completely.

I pushed the stylus a couple of inches away. I pushed the stylus away a couple of inches.

He backed ten feet off and waited. He backed off ten feet and waited.

I pulled half open both blinds. *I pulled open half both blinds.

He left the windows wide (completely) open. He left the windows open wide.

8. Example adapted from Spasov, p. 56.

He came part way down. He came down part way.

I left it partly in. I left it in partly.

He hammered the nail deep in. He hammered the nail in deep.

They traveled far away. They traveled away far.

He knocked the cap plumb off. *He knocked the cap off plumb.

He left his competitors miles behind.

It extends to expletives when used as intensifiers:

Turn that light the heck off.[9]

and it shows as somewhat less exceptional than it might otherwise appear the example cited by Fairclough (p. 48) using *distinctly* (compare *It is distinctly good = It is very good*):

You feel honoured that . . . they should bother to pick you distinctly out like that.

The particle (*a*)*way* has undergone a similar transformation to an intensive:

He took it way over to Animas County.

It flew way up in the sky.

It traveled way under the sea.

These modifications illustrate how easily elements that are intimately associated are reinterpreted as modifying one another or as functioning as units. *Back in, out back, up tight, down under,* and so on, are connected in ways that resemble compound prepositions.

The specialization of "back." The particle *back* has likewise undergone a specialization, stemming from a normal compounding of particles, for example,

He went out and then came back + He went out and then came in → He went out and then came back in.

The sense is extended to any "restoration of an original state" (Fraser, p. 84):

9. Fraser, p. 39.

I ripped the pocket but she sewed it back up.

They sold the property but then bought it back in.

It was so hot that I threw back off the covers.

"Restoration of a state" requires that the reference be to a resultant state, not primarily to an action:

The merchandise gave out, but they stocked it back up.

*They replenished the stock, but it gave back out.

The water flowed in and then leaked back out.

The plane took off, but then put back down (landed back).

*The plane landed and then took back off.

It was flattened, but it grew back up.

*He was heartened for a moment, but he gave back up.

They locked him up, but he got back out.

He got out, but they locked him back up.

*He escaped, but they picked him back up.

He threw it away, but later picked it back up.

*He recovered it, but later threw it back away.

Though *to dress down* and *to scold* are synonyms, there is no suggestion of resultant condition in the latter:

I thought he was going to behave himself but he didn't, and I had to dress him back down again.

*I thought he was going to behave himself but he didn't, and I had to scold him back again.[10]

Since *on* in one of its senses may be said to refer to a resultant condition (continuation) rather than a resultant state, an ambiguity results which makes the use of *back* with that sense unlikely except where the *on* phrase is fully specified:

?The avalanche was briefly checked, but then plunged back on.

10. The unacceptability of *scold back* is not because *scold* is a simple verb; witness

It emptied and I filled it back.

The letters were almost effaced, but I traced them back.

*They stopped a moment but soon went back on.

They stopped a moment but soon went back on their way.

He got off the wagon but soon got back on (literal "on").

When the reference is to action, the meaning is a particular kind of restoration, namely "requital" (there is a reciprocal action that evens the score):

I kissed her and she kissed me back.

I avoid hitting people because of the danger of being hit back.

Probably because of ambiguity with the other senses, *back* in this sense is not normally found coupled with other particles (Fraser, p. 82) or prepositional phrases:

*If you bawl me out I'll bawl you out back.

*He ran her down and she ran him down back.

*Don't punch in my nose or I'll punch in yours back.

*I voted against her and she voted against me back.

(If the prepositional phrase is a constituent separate from the verb, *back* can be used:

I looked at her and she looked back [at me].)

That ambiguity is the obstacle is suggested by the fact that when *right* is added there is no problem:

If you bawl me out I'll bawl you out right back.

I looked at her and she looked at me right back.

This *back* requires a little more informativeness in the object noun in order to precede it:

*She hit back the man.

Would you hit back an innocent person?

I'll even kiss back Jóhn if I have to.

(Compare the other *back*, which readily precedes:

She brought back the man.

Leave back in the contents.)

When there is neither action nor resultant state, that is, with stative meanings, *back* is unacceptable:

*I saw them and they saw me back.

*I owned this property once before and now I wish I owned it back.

*We hope that if we believe you, you will believe us back.

It is the nonstative meaning, however, and not the lexical label, that counts (see pp. 89–90):

They stole it from him and he wants it back.

I lost it but now I have it back (I have got it back).

Particles as nouns. The condition by which aspect-like or direction-like particles precede those that refer more to result probably reflects also—at least with the directional particles—a kind of prepositional phrase relationship in which the first particle functions as an adprep and the second as a sort of locative noun. Sentences like

He crawled in under.

They climbed up over.

can be interpreted as "He crawled into the under-space," "He climbed up through the over-space." But the terminal adverb in these cases is probably not to be viewed as a particle, any more than in

He climbed up on top.

They're sitting up front.

He came around in front.

He crawled down inside.

In other words, these are not properly combinations of particles. In

Let's go around back.

the *back* is locational, not directional, as can be seen in the possibility of preceding it with *in:*

Let's go around in back.

Also, these are doubtful candidates for the definite-noun-phrase test:

*He pushed in under the chairs.

?Bring around back the campstove.

Particles joined by conjunctions. Conjunctions with particles are used in two ways. One is for temporal sequence:

They came up and out.

He walked out and away.

They climbed over and down.

They turned around and back.

(This is not essentially different from a combination of particle and prepositional phrase. Spasov cites, p. 15, *Howard's eye flickered in my direction and then away again; She . . . walked quietly to the door and out.*) The other is intensive— for continuation or iteration. Not all the particles are regularly used in this way:

He wrote it over and over.

They went on and on (*along and along).

It soaked them through and through.

The bird flew up and up.

It fell down, down, down.

They flew away and away.

He kept running around and around (*about and about).

They worked it up and down.

He walked back and forth.

She runs in and out all day.

We note two restrictions here. One is semantic. The meanings of *in, by, aside, across,* and most other particles except the ones used in the examples are not amenable to "continuation" and consequently conjunctions of this kind are unusual:

?They pushed it in and in.

*He dragged himself across and across.

The other is a "binomial" type restriction that forbids reversing:

*He walked forth and back.

*She runs out and in.

*They worked it down and up.[11]

Cohesion of particle to particle. One highly predictable fact about multiple particles is that wherever one goes with respect to a direct object, the rest must go:

I tried to push back in the catchbolt.

*I tried to push back the catchbolt in.

They paddled the canoe back ashore.

*They paddled back the canoe ashore.

Bring on over your friends.

*Bring on your friends over.

If you shove back out the *A* folders, I'll look.

*If you shove back the *A* folders out, I'll look.

They brought back home the children.

*They brought back the children home.

The underbrush was thick, but we dragged the stuff up through nevertheless.

*The underbrush was thick, but we dragged up the stuff through, nevertheless.

If this were uniformly true, we might describe it by recognizing a single particle-position, which may move but may be "used" only once. But it does not hold for certain particles, notably the nautical ones. *Aboard,* for example, readily passes the definite-noun-phrase test and yet can be separated:

They pulled aboard the divers.

They pulled back the divers aboard.

They drew in the boat alongside.

He reeled in the catch astern.

They hauled in the catch ashore.

The same is true of *together:*

I stuck back the two halves together.

It is perhaps significant that these particles are the ones that

---

11. This example is acceptable in a meaning other than "iteration."

most resemble prepositional phrases, and that prepositional phrases are relatively free of the restriction (see p. 145):

*I tried to push back the catchbolt in.

I tried to push back the catchbolt in the lock.

*We dragged up the stuff through.

We dragged up the stuff through the underbrush.

If this fact is relevant, there would appear to be a tendency toward satisfying some vague condition of completeness where prepositional phrases are concerned. If there is already a prepositional phrase, or a particle resembling one, the condition is satisfied; if on the other hand there are two particles neither of which alone is a reasonable imitation of a prepositional phrase, the two must be combined as if one were a complement of the other. This tendency is facilitated by the *in under, up over* type (p. 140) and by the particular uses of *on, along,* and *back* already noted. Certain of the particles are virtual affixes—

Back home we had bacon every day.

Down South the weather is more muggy.

Was there any trouble *over your way?*

Up here it's more comfortable.

—and they appear to gravitate together in the same way with other particles. But some particles are more affixal than others—*back,* for example, is more so than *in,* as illustrated by two examples already cited:

*They paddled back the canoe ashore.

They hauled in the catch ashore.

The nonseparability of the particles gives further proof of the particle-like nature of certain adjectives:

He pushed back open the door.

*He pushed back the door open.

I tried to pull away loose the plastic covering.

*I tried to pull away the plastic covering loose.

But as a rule adjectives have no trouble being placed at the end separately from a preceding particle. Given a fairly intense semantic focus, this is true even of the cognate-object type:

She laced her bodice up tight.
?She laced up her bodice tight.
She laced up her bodice—tight.
She sweeps the floors off clean.
?She sweeps off the floors clean.
I wish for once you'd sweep off the floors clean!
He filled the barrel up full.
*He filled up the barrel full.
Can't you for God's sake fill up the barrel full?

Even under these best of conditions, it is virtually impossible to separate an adverbial particle:

?Try just this once to push up the piston through!

If possible at all, the emphasis is comparable to the quantifying modification exemplified in the next paragraph:

He pushed up the piston all the way through.

Where two particles side by side are unacceptable, they are also unacceptable separated, even though synonymous expressions may be acceptable:

They pushed off everything.
They pushed aside everything.
*They pushed off aside everything.
*They pushed off everything aside.
The pushed off everything to one side.
They split up the sticks.
They split apart the sticks.
*They split up apart the sticks.
*They split up the sticks apart.
They split up the sticks in half.

But if an end particle is modified by a quantifier it is acceptable. This is probably a special case of the semantic focus mentioned above:

They pushed up most of the stuff halfway through.
She scrubbed off the glass almost clean.
He wrote up the whole composition all over again.
He wrote up the whole composition twice over.
*He wrote up the whole composition over twice.
And in general there is no problem with prepositional phrases, though some are more usual than others and most are more comfortable with the particle and the preposition side by side (see pp. 162–163):
They hauled back the car over the ditch.
They pulled along the plow through the furrow.
We carried across the logs to the other side.
We took over the pie to our neighbors.
She brought along her mother to the concert.
Toss up a couple of rocks into my basket.
They tugged up the weight from below.
They let out the prisoners from the jail.
He stood up the pole against the wall.
?They drove back the cattle toward Abilene. (*See above for affixal "back."*)
The more or less stereotyped compound prepositions of course cannot be split:
*He took in the chairs to the house.
*They stuck on the posters to the wall.
This suggest viewing the restrictions in terms of relative compounding.
Unlike direct objects, manner adverbs may readily separate particles:
They brought back quickly in the damaged pieces.
He dashed on angrily ahead.
They came along slowly over.
The convoys were brought back steadily through.
It slid down gradually through.
He came up quietly forward.

CHAPTER 11

Added Elements

The effects of various kinds of insertions have up to this point been considered in the light of the two levels of stereotyping. The first level, that of phrasal verbs per se, was tested by inserting a simple definite noun phrase between particle and noun object. The moment the noun phrase is expanded and its potential information value increased, phrases that were rejected (and so defined as not phrasal verbs) become acceptable:

He did the job right.
*He did right the job.
He did right every one of his jobs.
She played her lovers false.
*She played false her lovers.
She played false the only truly faithful one of her lovers.

Second-level stereotypes were tested by insertions between verb proper and particle:

*A child grows quickly up.
?The states that make a nation up.
*He let a yell out.

But certain nonstereotypes, apparently because of conflict of homonyms, were found obliged to separate:

*She keeps up people.
She keeps people up.
She keeps up the membership.
*They put out the man.
They put the man out.
They put out the lights.

—unless, as with nonphrasal verbs, the noun phrase is expanded:

It's just that she keeps up so mány people with her racket that the whole neighborhood is down on her.

They put out the two men who were making a disturbance.

We are now interested in the nature of the insertions themselves and how connectedness in phrasal verbs is affected.

Manner adverbs. These have already been considered in relation to stereotypes and the separation of particles. It was found that the stereotyped combinations resist separation by a manner adverb, while others do not:

He ran the flag defiantly down (lowered it).

*He ran his friend defiantly down (in either sense).

Adverbial phrases in general, including those equivalent to manner adverbs, cannot (I think) be inserted even in non-stereotyped phrasal verbs:

*He pushed the gift with indifference away.

He pushed the gift indifferently away.

*I stumbled and fell while walking down. (for "fall down")

*She hurried on her way home along.

But they can be inserted in verb-adverb combinations that are not phrasal verbs:

The bird flew with boundless joy skyward.

*The bird flew with boundless joy up.

The bird flew joyfully up.

They loaded the stuff with all due care inside.

*They loaded the stuff with all due care in.

They loaded the stuff carefully in.

It drifted at random offside.

*It drifted at random off.

It drifted randomly off.

(The particles that resemble prepositional phrases [see pp. 142–143] show here the same half-independence as before:

?They lifted it with great skill aboard.

*They lifted it with great skill on.

They lifted it skillfully on.

?They waded with firm step ashore.

*They waded with firm step in.

They waded firmly in.)

It would appear from the examples that there is a formal restriction to -*ly* adverbs. But while this is possibly a necessary criterion, it is not a sufficient one. It is true that the adverbs *quick, fast,* and *slow* cannot be used (nor can *crosswise, underfoot, backwards, headlong,* and so on):

*They walked fast in.

They walked rapidly in.

*He tossed it quick up.

He tossed it quickly up.

*The procession moved slow on.

The procession moved slowly on.

*We laid it backwards down.

*He fell headlong down.

But the main criterion is that the adverb must belong to the familiar scalable or "degree" type. Thus we find no *so chemically, quite electrically, very immediately,* and the like, and we find *very scientifically* only in contexts where the primary "classificatory" meaning of *scientific* has yielded to an "evaluative" meaning. Hence

*He broke it scientifically down. (chemical analysis)

He cut it scientifically apart.

*They cut the molecules chemically apart.

They cut the molecules ingeniously apart.

*The magnet pulled it electrically back.

The magnet pulled it firmly back.

Within this general restriction, there is a narrower one that affects different phrasal verbs differently, according to the extent to which they are stereotyped. While an adverb such as *ingeniously* gives no trouble with the relatively unstereotyped *cut apart* (see above), it would be unacceptable in the relatively stereotyped *sew up*. On the other hand, an adverb such as *neatly* can readily be inserted:

  *She sewed it ingeniously up.

  She sewed it neatly up.

The criterion is the predictability and appropriateness of the adverb. The less predictable and appropriate it is, the more it will require the typical position assigned to unexpected elements: that of the main sentence accent at the end. So:

  He chopped it abruptly off.

  *He chopped it intentionally off.

  He chopped it off intentionally.

  We lighted the place brightly up.

  *We lighted the place abruptly up.

  We lighted the place up abruptly.

  He drank the liquid thirstily (avidly) down.

  *He drank the liquid obediently down.

  He drank the liquid down obediently.

  She held the gift graciously out.

  *She held the gift impersonally out.

  She held the gift out impersonally.

  He sat comfortably back.

  *He sat worriedly back.

  He sat back worriedly.

(Since almost any action can appropriately be hurried, *hurriedly* can replace the starred adverbs above without difficulty. The same is true, at least to some extent, of adverbs like *deftly*, *nicely*, and *neatly*.) This inner restriction relates to two phenomena already discussed. The first is the semantically cognate object type, in which the adjective is appropriate to the verb. Some comparisons:

  They planed smooth the boards.

They planed the boards smoothly down.
*They planed the boards easily down.
It ironed flat the foil.
It ironed the foil flatly out.
*It ironed the foil satisfactorily out.
She let loose her hair.
She let her hair loosely down.
*She let her hair furiously down.

The other is the intensive modifiers, which relate to the general perfectivity of phrasal verbs. The more readily a manner adverb can be viewed in a perfective sense, that is, the nearer it comes to being a synonym of *completely,* the easier it is to have an insertion even in comparatively stereotyped phrasal verbs. Thus *angrily* is certainly appropriate *to bawl out;* yet

*He bawled me angrily out.

is unacceptable, while

He bawled me thoroughly out.

is normal. Other pairs:

As far as interfering is concerned, I believe in holding religiously off.
* . . . in holding fervidly off.
As for the business, they took it fully over.
* . . . they took it efficiently over.
It was a stunning loss, but in time they made it scrupulously up.
* . . . they made it conscientiously up.
Hitler carried fanatically on with his plans.
*Hitler carried unexpectedly on with his plans.

Sentence adverbs. The degree (scalable) adverbs may function as sentence adverbs, modifying the proposition as a whole, or any major segment of it:

Gently he led the children over.
He gently led the children over.
*He led gently the children over.

He led the children gently over.

He led the children over gently.

But sentence adverbs which do not modify the proposition itself but the speaker's view of it (its truth or reality) behave differently. These "performatives" are comma insertions:

Hopefully, he led the children over.

He, hopefully, led the children over.

He led the children, hopefully, over.

He led the children over, hopefully.[1]

The effect of an insertion before the particle seems to be a kind of two-level discrimination. At the first level it divides particles that are clearly resultant *state* from the totality of resultant *condition,* and, of course, stereotypes of all kinds. In other words, if the particle refers to a terminus of motion, the adverb can be inserted; otherwise not:

We got it, luckily, out.

They shipped the stuff, apparently, back.

They fastened it, supposedly, together.

*He drove them, supposedly, along.

They left it, necessarily, open.

*They pulled it, necessarily, by.

*She stared him, presumably, down.

The same particle may or may not refer to a terminus of motion:

He got them, hopefully, through.

*They were carrying it, hopefully, through.

They had got us, fortunately, on, and we took our seats.

*The goal was unattainable, but they were impelling us, regrettably, on.

The second-level discrimination is between the phonetically bulkier and the phonetically less bulky particles. So, regardless

1. Degree adverbs, too, may be comma insertions, but are not required to be: *The master, gently and fondly, led the children over.*

of the favorable context ("success" verb *get* plus terminus of motion), one is unlikely to find

*It's a long stairway, but we'll get you, hopefully, up.
but one readily finds

You will take it, necessarily, home.
Most of the examples cited are to some degree doubtful, but the difference in degree of acceptability favors, I think, the explanation given. This is confirmed by the readiness with which the set of particles resembling prepositional phrases accepts the insertion:

They brought us, fortunately, ashore.

He was taken, presumably, aboard.

You would attach them, theoretically, together.
The same particles are the ones which combine with *to be* in the sense of result. In the last set of examples, we are ashore, they are aboard, and they are together.

The effect of length on such insertions is of course not peculiar to this aspect of phrasal verbs—it partly underlies the definite-noun-phrase test—nor even to phrasal verbs in general, but is found in complements of other kinds and must be regarded as a general fact of English word order:

?They will make you, presumably, act.

They will make you, presumably, readjust.

?You will find them, hopefully, glad.

You will find them, hopefully, enthusiastic.

Overlapping stereotypes. I introduce this paragraph to speculate on two curious examples:

. . . places you might be interested in looking further up.[2]

I walk barefoot around.[3]

I surmise that the first represents an overlapping of *to look*

2. *Places* means "references." The speaker was John W. Carr, III, of the University of North Carolina, 15 February 1963.
3. Nineteen-year-old speaker.

further and *to look up,* the second an overlapping of *to walk barefoot* and *to walk around.* I would guess that this is the case rather than an independent assembling of *look + further + up* and *walk + barefoot + around,* or at least that it has influenced the latter.

Sentential insertions. The relevant insertions are object noun clauses and adjective clauses modifying object nouns. The former have already been discussed (Chapter 9). Adjective clauses introduced by relative words allow the particle to stand directly before or directly after. The relative *that,* which when not a subject is often dropped in English, is more apt to be retained when the particle precedes:

They brought the stuff over that I wanted.

They brought the stuff (that) I wanted over.

They pushed the legislation through that was needed.

They pushed the legislation that was needed through.

They auctioned the place off where we used to live.

They auctioned the place (where) we used to live off.

End position of the particle is restricted in the same way as with sentential objects. If it goes too far to the right it seems to be "lost," and this is complicated generally by ambiguity.[4] Contexts and particles vary in the degree of ambiguity. *Up* is the most difficult to place at the end, even in a literal sense; the sensation is of something phonologically too insubstantial to stand alone:

He brought the dishes up that we had been waiting for.

?He brought the dishes (that) we had been waiting for up.

They led the man away who had done the most for them.

---

4. Poutsma (p. 422) felt ambiguity to be a factor here. Henry Sweet (*A New English Grammar, Logical and Historical* [Oxford, Clarendon Press, 1898], sec. 1843) also appealed to ambiguity, but to explain our reluctance to say *I have left behind my umbrella,* he said that "the adverb might be mistaken for a preposition."

They led the man who had done the most for them away.

Don't throw any of the stuff out that I want to keep.

*Don't throw any of the stuff (that) I want to keep out.

Let's look that place over where we used to live.

*Let's look that place where we used to live over.

They put the lights out that were too bright.

*They put the lights that were too bright out.[5]

They threw the fellows out who were too boisterous.

They threw the fellows who were too boisterous out.

It is almost a foregone conclusion that examples with *look over* and *put out* will not be acceptable because of the stereotype. But *lead away* and *throw out* are clearly literal resultant condition and nevertheless the examples differ, presumably because *were too boisterous out* and *do something for them away* are not ambiguous (only nonsensical), while *keep out* creates a conflict. This is confirmed by the relatively greater acceptability of

Don't throw any of the stuff (that) I want to keep ready out.

We also find degrees of clarity where resultant condition is concerned. We might expect an adjective to fare better in end position than an adverbial particle, and it seems to do so:

I expect you to wipe clean (wipe off) every tool (that) you take before you hand it back.

I expect you to wipe every tool clean (off) that you take before you hand it back.

5. How much the unacceptability here is a matter of degree can be shown by the freedom the speaker has to alter certain of the gradient elements of the prosody, particularly accent and disjuncture, to clear up the ambiguity and make an example such as this acceptable. If *the lights that were too bright* is already known from the context, so that the hearer accepts it as a unit and the only newly introduced item is the verb *put out*, by widening and disjuncture before *out* and emphasizing *out* strongly the sentence becomes normal. The semantic focus is on *out*.

I expect you to wipe every tool (that) you take clean (?off)
   before you hand it back.

(That ambiguity is not the only factor is suggested by the
fact that the last example—despite the ambiguity of *take off*—
is not improved by replacing *take* with *borrow*.) Whether because of length or of ambiguity, a reduced clause seems to favor
end position of the particle more than one in which the relative
and the verb are retained:

   ?They left the pieces that had the rough corners out.
   They left the pieces with the rough corners out.
   *She had a dress that was three sizes too big on.
   She had a dress three sizes too big on.
   ?We brought clothing that was heavier than we needed
      along.
   We brought clothing heavier than we needed along.
   ?They shipped the portrait that is like the one you have
      back.
   They shipped the portrait like the one you have back.
   ?Why did they take the stuff that was in the parlor away?
   Why did they take the stuff in the parlor away?

Reduced clauses appear to accept mid position of the particle
to the extent that they are, or embody, post-modifier phrases,
but not if they are single words:

   I checked the stars off visible to the naked eye.
   *I checked the stars off visible.
   We took the diamonds back stolen from the jewelry store.
   *We took the diamonds back stolen.
   They hauled the goods away left in storage.
   *They hauled the goods away stored.[6]
   We took supplies along in the form of implements and
      victuals.

6. Acceptable, of course, in an irrelevant sense.

We took supplies along of implements and victuals.

We took supplies along quite unusable.

*We took supplies along unusable.

I left the door open to your grandmother's room.

(It goes without saying that adjectives which are themselves complements of the phrasal verb are not affected:

I turned the light on bright.)

But if there is a suggestion of an adverbial element in the adjective, the one-word condition falls. This occurs with certain locational participles, including a few that occasionally commute with prepositions, e.g. *the room adjoining yours = the room beside (next to) yours, the day following the accident = the day after the accident:*

I left the door open adjoining. (Compare "alongside.")

We took the day off following. (succeeding)

I wrote the data up attached.

Would you check the pages off enclosed?

The condition also falls when the noun is an item of extremely low semantic content. So we say *everything nice, something hot, nothing new,* and so forth, and are more likely to say *A man angry is not to be trifled with* than to say **The politician angry was calmed down,* where *man* is relatively empty to begin with and is made more so in the indefinite phrase *a man.* So:

They carted everything off cartable.

Don't throw anything away useful.

The police brought the men in involved, but there was little else they could do.

Leave any stuff behind unlabeled.

Relative clauses with *as* behave like adjective clauses with other relatives. All three positions are possible:

They took in as many refugees as they dared.

They took as many refugees in as they dared.

They took as many refugees as they dared in.

Excessive length "loses" the particle:

I brought as many parts as I could spare over.

*I brought as many parts as I could spare from my own stock over.

Ambiguity is a factor:

We threw away as much stuff as we kept.

We threw as much stuff away as we kept.

*We threw as much stuff as we kept away.

Sentential modifiers incorporated in clauses with *-ever* allow no middle position but seem to behave like the foregoing with end position:

Take whatever models show defects apart.

*Take whatever models apart show defects.

I expect you to wipe whatever tools you use clean (?off).

Bring whichever one you prefer in.

?We'll lay whatever gift you decide on for your children aside.

But insertions tend to be shorter, and perhaps ambiguity is more readily tolerated:

I'll take whoever comes along. (for "take along")

Sentential modifiers in the form of *-ing* phrases tend to be ambiguous when the particle precedes the *-ing* form, and this position is less likely. End position is avoided as before if the particle is "lost":

They led away demonstrators wearing McCarthy buttons.

?They led demonstrators away wearing McCarthy buttons.

They led demonstrators wearing McCarthy buttons away.

Take apart any models showing defects.

?Take any models apart showing defects.

Take any models showing defects apart.

I'd like to bring along all the candidates meeting the requirements.

?I'd like to bring all the candidates along meeting the
   requirements.

?I'd like to bring all the candidates meeting the requirements
   along.

Sentential modifiers in the form of infinitive phrases allow
all three positions, but length and ambiguity again are factors
in mid and final position:

We'll vote in the first person to reach 75.

We'll vote the first person in to reach 75.

We'll vote the first person to reach 75 in.

Take apart any models to show defects.

?Take any models apart to show defects.

?Take any models to show defects apart.

We were reading through the last novel to be published.

*We were reading the last novel through to be published.

?We were reading the last novel to be published through.

If there is a change of subject, length is increased and end
position becomes more doubtful:

I think I've ferreted out the one for you to call your own.

I think I've ferreted the one out for you to call your own.

*I think I ferreted the one for you to call your own out.

We handed over the money for them to spend.

We handed the money over for them to spend.

*We handed the money for them to spend over.

There are doubtless other varieties of adjective modification
that could be cited, but I see no reason to expect any startling
differences from the ones illustrated. It is obvious that rather
highly flexible processes of "surface" adjustment are involved.
Tolerance of a far-removed particle, for example, is unstable
from speaker to speaker and probably from occasion to occasion. The following citation would strike most readers as awkward even though it is justified by the fact that the noun phrase
refers to something known from the context:

> Although we have not ruled the use of other visual devices
> of an electromechanical nature out, until some of these
> devices . . . [7]

A more important qualification is that observations on insertions with phrasal verbs will remain incomplete until the larger
question of all such insertions is dealt with. I have presented
relative clauses, for example, as affecting phrasal verbs, when
it may turn out that a better focus is how phrasal verbs affect
relative clauses. This will be true if we find that the particles
of phrasal verbs behave in this respect essentially as other adverbs or similar complements behave:

They had on hand the stuff that they needed.
They had the stuff on hand that they needed.
They had the stuff that they needed on hand.
We named chairman that woman with the flower in her
hat.
We named that woman chairman with the flower in her
hat.
We named that woman with the flower in her hat chairman.
I found the diamonds today stolen from the jewelry store.
*I found the diamonds today stolen. (starred in the relevant
sense "that were stolen")
I opened the door again adjoining.
*I copied the data again attached.
We'll cart everything here cartable.
I took from my own stock as many parts as I could spare.
I took as many parts from my own stock as I could spare.
I took as many parts as I could spare from my own stock.
I'll take gladly whoever comes.
I'll take whoever comes, gladly.

7. *A Self-Instructional Course in Brazilian Portuguese,* USOE project
first-phase report, 1 February 1963, p. 22.

I'd like to bring with me all the candidates meeting the requirements.

I'd like to bring all the candidates with me meeting the requirements.

I'd like to bring all the candidates meeting the requirements with me.

Pack carefully any models to show defects.

*Pack any models carefully to show defects.

Pack any models to show defects carefully.

We hope to pick soon the time for you to come.

We hope to pick the time soon for you to come.

We hope to pick the time for you to come soon.

By and large there seems to be nothing special about phrasal verbs in these constructions, particularly as the over-all lengthening makes it possible to have almost any complement directly after the verb, which normally is true only with phrasal verbs: *They had on hand the stuff that they needed* is normal, **They had on hand the stuff* is not. This makes the positioning of particles and the positioning of other complements pretty much the same. There is probably more freedom than with particles to place other complements at the end: *I took as many parts as I could spare from my own stock* is ambiguous, but this causes no trouble in either of the two senses. One reason no doubt is the relatively greater phonetic bulk of the nonparticle complements. It is easier to vary the accents and disjunctures with an element like *from my own stock* (or even a single, but readily accentable, item like *soon*) than with one such as *out* or *up:* ?*I took as many parts as I could spare out*. Signaling the constituents is correspondingly simplified. Another reason is the predicative adjunct nature of the particle, which keeps it more as a direct satellite of the noun.

To generalize as best one can: the particle may stand next to the verb, between the noun with its pre-modifiers if any and its post-modifiers, or following the noun phrase. Ambiguity is a factor in mid position and both ambiguity and length in end position. The latter illustrates a sort of German-style "bracketing" of the noun phrase by the phrasal verb.

Additions to the particle. Examples of quantitative modifiers added to the particle have already been noted (see pp. 135–137). The expected effect is that the news value of the particle will be increased to the point that it will require end position unless there is some concomitant augmentation of another element:

He took off his leggings.
*He took completely off his leggings.
We pulled up the blinds.
*We pulled six inches up the blinds.
Lower down the elevator.
*Lower a mite farther down the elevator.
Lower a mite farther down the smaller of the two elevators.
Where the quantifier modifies the phrasal verb as a whole, this effect does not occur:

*He had taken partly off his leggings.
He had partly taken off his leggings.
*He let half out the water.
He half let out the water.
(Unless the particle has its literal value, a quantifier cannot be used except to modify the phrasal verb as a whole:

*He let a yell half out.
*He let half out a yell.
He half let out a yell.)
It is probably impossible to have a personal pronoun after a modified particle:

He sewed completely up both tears.
*You'll have to sew completely up him.
Adding more than one particle to the same verb affects the prosody in the same way as modifying the particle:

Push in the switch. Push out the switch.

*Push in or out the switch.

It can be worked by pushing in or out a sort of double-action switch.

Additions after the particle. A corollary to the nonseparation of particles when more than one occur in the same sentence is the tendency, under the same conditions, for a particle and a locational-directional phrase to stay together. Since the phrase cannot be inserted in the bracketing but must stay at the end, the result is that the particle tends to be pulled there too. Van Dongen exemplifies (p. 346):

She turned her face away from the others.

She put her hat on over it all.[8]

It is probably the affinity of *up* and *there* in *up there* that makes the following example sound awkward nowadays:

Towards evening, Mr. Pen would stroll in the direction of his club, and take up Warrington there for a constitutional walk.[9]

Other examples:

I brought my friends along to the party.

?I brought along my friends to the party.

I sent my family off to California.

?I sent off my family to California.

Take the groceries in through the back door.

?Take in the groceries through the back door.

The questioned examples are all acceptable, but a shade less likely than the others, particularly in cases like these where the particle has its literal meaning. If there is a stereotype, the particle may be held next to the verb, for example,

8. Van Dongen lists (pp. 109, 121) other examples, such as *I leave the decision up to you.*
9. *Pendennis*, p. 435.

He brought back his Peugeot from France.

He brought his Peugeot back from France.

The first suggests that he acquired it there—*bring back* is existential and *Peugeot* is introduced on the scene. This shows more clearly in an example that is a bit ridiculous in any other sense:

He brought back a wife from France.

?He brought a wife back from France.

Nevertheless, adding to the particle improves many strikingly peculiar displacements:

*He let a curse out.

He let a curse out on mankind and the universe in general.

*They put studying off.

They put studying off to another time.

*Don't let who you are on.

?Don't let who you are on to anybody.

*Didn't you promise to give smoking up?

Didn't you promise to give smoking up for the time being?

The last two examples raise the question of how essential it is for the addition to be locational-directional. It is not surprising that compound prepositions like *away from* and *off to* should resist separation, but there is more to it than this. There is the information value of the augmented particle. The example

*We brought clothing that was heavier than we needed along.

was unmotivated because *clothing that was heavier than we needed* is clearly the semantic focus. But in

We brought clothing that was heavier than we needed along to California.

the news value of *to California* may well tip the scales. In this more general way—merely the addition of something *after* the particle, whether part of a compound preposition involving the particle[10] (this is the strongest case) or an adverb or a prepositional phrase or an adjective clause—supposedly difficult postpositions of the particle become normal or at least less strange. It would not be necessary to labor the point were it not for the frequent starring of examples like *He let a yell out* not to indicate *unacceptability* but *ungrammaticality*—it is assumed that there is a grammatical rule preventing the break-up of *to let out* rather than a rule of sentence dynamics which governs—rather flexibly—the conditions under which the break-up may occur. In many if not most stereotypes there is enough information value left in the particle to permit a postposition if this postposition is not the extreme one of end position. So:

*They let what had happened out.

They let what had happened out of the bag.

*She takes washing in.

She takes washing in regularly.

*They found the truth out.

They found the truth out just in time.

?I expect you to wipe every tool that you take off before you hand it back.

I expect you to wipe every tool that you take off carefully before you hand it back.

*He put the decision he had been considering off.

He put the decision he had been considering off for the moment.

*Take that problem I raised up.

Take that problem I raised up with the manager.

*He let a yell out.

He stood at the top of that hill and let a yell out that could be heard in the next county.

---

10. Or some similar case like
*She sweeps off the floors clean.
She sweeps off the floors clean as a whistle.

*He let a string of oaths fly.

He let a string of oaths fly that had my ears burning.

*She let a couple of snide remarks fall.

She let a couple of snide remarks fall that had the whole social register in an uproar for a week.

The tightness of the stereotype still affects the result. The verb *to take in,* for example, in the sense "enjoy," is tightly bound in *to take in the sights* but somewhat more loosely bound when the object is some other form of spectacle-type entertainment. Hence

Let's take in the sights.

*Let's take the sights in.

?What do you say we take some of the sights in this afternoon?

Let's take in a movie.

*Let's take a movie in.

What do you say we take a couple of movies in this afternoon?

At another level the verb *to take up* with a sport or occupation as its object is a rather firmly stereotyped existential verb—the sport or occupation is introduced on the scene:

He took up the study of law.

He took up golf.

*He took golf up.

—adding something is not much of an improvement:

?He took golf up after he was sixty years old.

But when the stereotype is broken (or at least bent) by concretizing the abstract noun, postposition is more acceptable:

When are you going to take your golf up again?

This example recalls the earlier observations on familiarity and expectedness (Chapter 4).

Additional verbs. Transitive phrasal verbs may be conjoined with one another or with simple verbs. The usual effect is to make the particle and the verb inseparable:

He signed and handed over the report.
*He signed and handed the report over.
They bought up and resold the property.
He filled out and handed in the questionnaire.

Poutsma felt (p. 421) that this inseparability held invariably. But there is at least one exception, namely two verbs (or the same verb repeated) having the same particle:

I would pull and tug and yank that stuff out no matter how tough it was.

We've counted and counted those figures up so many times we've lost track.

Whether there exists any other possibility besides this type of iteration (*pull, yank,* and *tug* are semantic repetitions) I do not know. Afterthoughts and emendations on the part of a speaker would be hard to formulate:

I'd either lock, or better still, séal that house up if I were away. There are too many burglars around.

Elsewhere, with particles and verbs inevitably having different relationships to each other, it appears that the binding effect is stable:

Whether you take up or give up a sport is a matter of time and money.

*Whether you take or give up a sport . . .

*Whether you take or give a sport up . . .

Can't we shake off or hold off the pursuers?

*Can't we shake or hold off the pursuers?[11]

*Can't we shake or hold the pursuers off?

To report successive actions, it is doubtful that a particle can

---

11. Possibly acceptable to a speaker who admits *shake* in this sense without *off*. A similar case is Spasov's example (p. 15) *I'll drink this off and be off,* which he cites to show the fusion of verb and particle. *I'll drink this and be off* is of course normal because *drink* does not require *off.*

even be repeated, much less postposed:

I brought out and aired the flag.

*I brought out and shook out the flag.

They dragged in and deposited the trunks.

*They dragged in and left in the trunks.

He picked up and threw the ball.

*He picked up and tossed up the ball.

But the repetition is possible for more or less concurrent or repeated actions. The last example is acceptable if viewed in this way. Similarly

I've got to think up and work up a topic.

They herded in and drove in and pushed in the rebellious animals.

Note for iteration of successive actions:

*He took up and gave up golf.

He took up and gave up golf, took up and gave up tennis, took up and gave up swimming—never could settle down to a single sport.

CHAPTER 12

Dative Objects

Thus far no examples have involved the presence of an indirect object in the verb phrase. I have only one—not very clear—example of a prepositionless dative without any accompanying direct object:[1]

> I'll tell Janet to call you down right away. (call down to you)

The clear examples all involve a combination of direct and indirect objects. Three situations need to be considered: when the indirect object is a pronoun, when it is a noun, and when it is either a noun or a pronoun preceded by a preposition.

Poutsma believed (p. 421) that a dative pronoun forced the particle to precede the direct object:

> He poured me out a glass.
> *He poured me a glass out.

The unacceptability of the last example, however, rests on other grounds:

> Are you going to póur me a glass of that stuff óut or aren't you?
> Just póur me a gláss óut and I'll táste it.

The difficulty is not one of order exclusively, but of order conjugating with accent in conveying various weights of information. Poutsma's example is unmotivated: *glass* is a measure word which is either informative (not previously mentioned) or not informative at all. In either case it is most likely at the end—first, accented, second, unaccented. An *indefinite* measure word can comfortably occupy the interior position which

---

1. Said unconsciously by myself.

is one of lower but not zero or maximum information:

He poured me some out.

Besides, Poutsma's example is not really ungrammatical. With accent deletion on items except the verb proper,

I never expected him to póur you a glass out.

or with sufficient weight of information on the verb, as in the preceding examples with accent on *out* and in

After all the fuming and fussing he simply poured me a glass óut and that was that.

it is perfectly acceptable. We see how easy it is to be distracted by something irrelevant—in this case the measure word—if we compare instances where the distraction is absent:

She gave me back the letter. She gave me the letter back.

Take him his coat along when you go.

If you'll dish us that stuff out now, we can eat and get going.

It seems safe to say that the dative pronoun virtually has to precede the particle, regardless of the position of the direct object:

I want you to hand me it down right now.[2]

Run me this off. Run me off this.

Write me out the recipe.

Reach me that over.

Bring us up a couple of sandwiches.

End position of the pronoun is barely conceivable, under the most intense semantic focus:

I can't imagine them bringing up mé anything as nice as that.

When the indirect object is a noun, it still tends to precede

---

2. *Me* is the only pronoun that shows maximum possibilities. There are curious restrictions with the other pronouns: *We want you to hand us it down right now.* Mitchell cites (p. 105) *Hand me it down.*

the particle:
> Take your friends out some watermelon slices.
> *Take out your friends some watermelon slices.
> Hand these fellows down as many copies as they want.
> Hand these fellows as many copies down as they want.
> ?Hand down these fellows as many copies as they want.
> Write your friend out that recipe.
> *Write out your friend that recipe.
> Bring your friend one of thóse over.

But the balance here is more nearly even, and a very close-knit phrasal verb can precede the indirect object as a unit:
> Pack your brother up a nice lunch.
> Pack up your brother a nice lunch.

This is particularly true when the indirect object is weighted:
> Bring over these friends of yours some of that shish kebob.
> Bring up any people you want as many things as you want.

When the indirect object is introduced by a preposition, the result seems to be no different from that of the additional modification already noted (Chapter 11):
> *They held both plays in both theaters over.
> They held both plays in both theaters over for us.
> See if you can scare up a méal.
> *See if you can scare a méal up.
> See if you can scare a méal up for us somewhere.

and no different from an interpolated adverb phrase anywhere else:
> He brought both the manager and the secretary-treasurer in with him.
> He brought in with him both the manager and the secretary-treasurer.
> *He brought in with him the manager.
> They held over for us both plays in both theaters.
> *They held over for us the play.

CHAPTER 13

Unfinished Business

The residue of topics left untouched in a subject as encompassing as phrasal verbs is certain to be larger than the number treated. I purposely limited the field by omitting certain combinations—notably verb plus preposition; and I omitted certain approaches to the combinations that were included, such as the statistics of the lexicon. But there are many more questions that deserve to be studied. A few are discussed below.

Generalizations about meaning. Are there things that can be said about phrasal verbs as a class, or about large segments of them, that set them apart from one-word verbs? It is not likely that any clear-cut distinction will emerge, but there are probably significant differences. For example, a semantic feature of "intentionality" has been noted for certain verbs as against others. Thus

Why don't you see it?

would (unless *see* is taken as *go see*) have to be answered by something like *I am not able to*. But

Why don't you look at it?

would expect something like *I don't want to*. This feature seems to be a common or at least widespread property of phrasal verbs as against the synonymous simple verbs. In the following examples the parenthesis is an answer relatively more appropriate to the question:

Why don't you pass our house? (The road goes the other way.)

Why don't you pass by our house? (I will if you want me to.)

Why don't you choose a nice one? (I can't find any.)

Why don't you pick out a nice one? (It's kind of you to offer.)

Why don't you examine him? (He never comes to my office.)
Why don't you look him over? (It's a good idea; I think
I will.)
Why don't you leave? (There's no bus at this hour.)
Why don't you go away? (I'd like to, but they won't let
me.)

For the last two examples, compare the doubtful *?Why don't
you leave and stop bothering me?* and the fully acceptable
Why don't you go away and stop bothering me? Where *why
don't you?* cannot be interpreted as either invitation (to an
intentional act) or as inquiring about someone's custom (a
durative act), the result is unacceptable:

*Why don't you overtake John?
Why don't you catch up with John?
?Why don't you enter? (acceptable in reference to a contest)
Why don't you go in?

The feature of intentionality cannot be viewed as an absolute,
and this raises the question of gradience. The examples

He deliberately discarded it.
He deliberately threw it away.

are both correct, but the element of intention is stronger in
the phrasal verb.

Questions of register. Proportionately more phrasal verbs,
and fewer polymorphemic one-word verbs, are informal. We
need answers to the following: Is most nontechnical verb formation[1] done with phrasal verbs? Are phrasal verbs and their
derivatives strikingly more frequent in spoken than in written
English? (A *yes* answer spells drastic consequences for dictionary making.) Is there a literary lag where splitting phrasal
verbs is concerned? (This is suggested in an example like

---

1. Other than zero formation, i.e., direct shift of part of speech: *a
pad, to pad.* But note *to pad out* and also *They padded down with her*
as an immediately transparent coinage.

I know you're acting from the best of motives. But you
want me to let off Scarborough, partly because you know
his father, partly . . .[2]

where Scarborough is the subject of the conversation and would
expect a less contrastive position.) What is the proportion of
phrasal verbs in specialized vocabularies, for example, hip jar-
gon? Does register affect the kinds of meanings that are normally tied to phrasal verbs? (Intentionality, for example, is
more to be expected in informal than in critical and scientific
language.)

Neology in phrasal verbs. Some kinds of word making are
deliberate (*to adsorb, to pneumatize*), others are unconscious
but still distinct, in the rules they apply and the results they
achieve, from free syntactic composition (*to outbuild, to airlift*), and still others are at the borderline between free combination into phrases and less-than-free combination into words.
Phrasal verbs should be ideal for establishing contrasts in this
domain, for they range from combinations with little or no
trace of bondage (*to airlift off the merchandise, to airlift out
the merchandise, to airlift back the merchandise,* and so on)
to indivisible compounds (*to make out a tax form, to make
up a questionnaire, to make off in a hurry*). The looseness
of the structures not only makes combining easier but also permits other mechanisms of word formation to operate more
freely—the existence of the verb *to black out* referring to tex-
tual deletions made *to white out* inevitable through analogy
the moment a suitable white preparation was marketed. Studies
should be made of spontaneous creation, and acceptability tests
devised to see how readily speakers accept mildly or strongly
unexpected combinations—to find for example whether sentences like

2. J. C. Masterman, *An Oxford Tragedy* (London, Victor Gollancz, Ltd.,
1934), p. 14.

> The job these girls do is stroking up the hairs to make the furs presentable.
>
> The cop gave me no chance to explain; he cited me in and that was that.

would be understood and accepted without question, or noticed as peculiar. Some of the specific questions related to the more general problem can be illustrated with the particle *up* used in denominal and deadjectival verbs with the sense "to provide with (whatever the noun or adjective designates)":

> Be sure to flour up the board before you try to knead the dough on it.
>
> Feather up the arrows.
>
> Let's gas up and get going.
>
> I haven't finished graphing up these figures.

These are clearly "perfective," as we expect of the particle *up*. But is *up* also being used as a sort of verb-forming affix, like *-ate*, for example, *to page up = to paginate?* Or does the word to which *up* is attached have to be a verb already? This would seem to be at least partly true, if restrictions with colors are to be explained:

> Let's green up the landscape a bit in the background of our picture.
>
> *Let's red (blue, pink, brown) up . . .

—*green* and *black* are fairly common as verbs, the other colors are less so except in special senses. (Compare also *to gas up, to fuel up,* and *to coal up.*) Is the process more or less limited to monosyllables? (*To purple up, to scarlet up, to orange up,* and *to gasoline up* would be hard to take.)

Neology in deverbal nouns. Perhaps the most productive device for making deverbal nouns is the simple stress-shift in forms like *spín-off, rúbdown, púshover, knóckout, leád-in, fláreup, fádeaway, púllback, cóme-on, bréakthrough, túrnabout, gítalong, rúnaround, gó-by, gét-together, gó-ahead*—to illustrate with as wide a choice of particles as possible. The relative freedom with which these forms appear makes them a good testing ground for the same kinds of questions as those raised in the preceding section, and also for the nature of the semantic specialization that accompanies the creation of such a form. Subjects could be tried with previously unfamiliar nouns based on familiar phrasal verbs, for example,

That was a real lúckout you had, fellow.

Where are you going on your next shóveoff?

to find the degree of acceptability, to elicit definitions, and the like. Companion tests on forms without the shift of stress could tell us how extensive this form of simple zero derivation is (*Only a frantic wriggle lóose saved the cub from the trap. It was a regular knock dówn and drag óut at that party*)[3] and how the resulting forms match the verbs on the one hand and the stress-shifted nouns on the other in sense. An allied question is the extent to which nouns of the same type are generated without an existing verb, for example, the *sick in* or *sick out* used (1970) of workers reporting sick instead of overtly striking.

Lexical surveys. No large-scale count of phrasal particles and verbs entering into phrasal combinations has been made, so far as I know.[4] One is reported in preparation, by Adam Makkai at the University of Illinois, using a computer to study occurrences of one thousand simple verbs in combination with thirty-two particles.[5] Some tentative confirmations have already emerged, for example the preponderance of words of Germanic origin, the top-rank productivity of *up,* the predictability of

3. See Bolinger, "Ambiguities in Pitch Accent," *Word* 17:309–317 (1961) for additional examples.
4. M. A. K. Halliday, in "Class in Relation to the Axes of Chain and Choice," *Linguistics* 2:5–15 (1963), mentioned (p. 11) a computational study of phrasal verbs, but I am not aware that it has been completed.
5. The information on this point comes from Makkai, "The Two Idiomaticity Areas in English and Their Membership: A Stratificational View," *Linguistics* 50:44–58 (1969), esp. pp. 55–57.

a high frequency of idiomatic combinations if a particle has a high frequency of literal ones, and the proportion of actual forms to potentially occurring ones (in a sample of 100 verbs and 25 particles, there are 20,000 possibilities; 1,054 were actually found in such a sample). A study of this type will give us a good deal of valuable information, but others are needed to supplement it. For example, circumscribing in advance the particles that are to be counted leaves untouched one of the most interesting problems: what words can serve as the nonverbal partners of verbs in making phrasal verbs. We have seen that among the adverbs those related to seafaring are a sizable segment, and that besides adverbs it is necessary to include adjectives and a few infinitives; it is important to know how far this widening of the pattern extends. Does it include nouns? One wonders because of the parallel in

They were at outs but they finally made up.

They were at outs but they finally made friends.

We made out with what we had.

We made shift with what we had.

(*Make friends* and *make shift,* being intransitive, are hard to test; but they do not seem to allow splitting:

I wish they'd make the hell up.

*I wish they'd make the hell friends.)

What we need is an idiom dictionary that excludes nothing on the basis of a prior definition of what a phrasal verb or other set combination is beyond the fact that it is partially or wholly stereotyped in meaning. Besides guiding us in deciding what to count, such a dictionary would help in calculating the proportion of all verb senses carried by phrasal verbs, in determining how stable the meanings of the particles are and how they are interrelated, in making better distinctions between pure prepositions and other particles, and so on.

Problems in grammatical theory. The earlier generative treatments of phrasal verbs obviously need revision. *To bring the letter back* is not an optional transformation of *to bring back the letter*—both orders must be attributed to some element of focus in deep structure. And the position of the pronoun in *take him on* is a statistic, not the result of an obligatory transformation. These are minor questions, affecting only the phrasal verbs themselves. A broader one is that of divided or indeterminate constituency—of what goes with what. We have seen this in two different forms. The first is the over-lapped compound preposition that was labled *adprep*. In *He ran up the hill* the single word *up* is both adverb to the verb and preposition to the noun—the functions can be divided exactly as with two-word compound prepositions:

He ran *up.—Up* what?

He ran *away.—From* where?

To accommodate this it may be necessary to revive the concept of the portmanteau, giving it the sense of a morphological rather than a phonemic overlap. In deep structure the adverbial and the prepositional elements would appear separately, with a fusing transformation applied wherever they are identical. The still largely untested approach of generative semantics should find a question of this sort fruitful, for it predicts such morphological fusions of semantically separate elements. An "up up" embodied in an *up* is no more strange than a "cause to become hard" embodied in a *harden* or a "become not alive" embodied in a *die*. The main difference with *up up* is that the fusion is almost purely structural and has little to do with semantic features. This is to say that in "become not alive" we have a verb feature, an adverb (negation) feature, and an adjective feature rolled into one, but each element is also semantically distinct; in "up up" there is an adverb feature and a preposition feature, but the two are not easily separated semantically. Perhaps one could say "in an upward direction" for one and "along the upward course of" for the other, but this seems a bit forced.

The second constituency problem illustrates this more sharply. It is the affinity of the particle in sentences like *Take off your shoes,* where one is hard put to decide whether it belongs more to the verb proper or to the noun—the action is one of doffing, and the result is shoes that are off. (It is precisely this indeterminacy that allows adjectives into the pattern—*to cut open the melon* is to open the melon by cutting it, and to cut the melon in such a way that it is open; and the same indeterminacy is confirmed in the mobility of the particle—now associated with the verb, now with the noun.) As with *up,* we could have recourse to doubling in the underlying sentence—one *off* to go with *take,* the other to serve as a predicate of an embedded sentence:

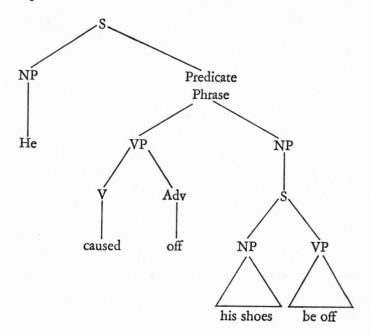

But such an underlying structure is redundant in a way we would prefer not to have it. An underlying "He caused his shoes to be off" is readily transformable to "He caused off his shoes," with a surface structure of *He removed his shoes,* but this "uses up" the *off. He took off his shoes* retains the *off* in double function (it is as explicit as **He removed his shoes off*), with semantic identity but structural fusion—adverb plus predicate complement. A possible solution would be to distinguish *He took off his shoes* from *He took his shoes off* by construing *off* as an adverb in the first and as a predicate complement in the second. But that would be feasible only if the word order responded solely to this structural contrast; instead there are additional factors—contrastive pointing, length, and so on, as we have seen. The problem of multiple or indefinite constituency is a difficult one and is probably more common than is generally thought.[6]

6. I give a couple of illustrations from outside the sphere of phrasal verbs. Take the sentence
He likes everybody—he even manages to like Bill.
It has been claimed that *even* is an immediate constituent of *Bill*. See R. A. Hudson, "The Use of Linkers," in R. D. Huddleston et al., *Sentence and Clause in Scientific English;* preliminary ed. (London, 1968), p. 358. So it is, in a way, and the distribution of the accents (as with *He ónly has tén*) seems to mark the two words as partners. But the position indicates something else: *even* goes where it goes because the sentence also means "It is true that he likes everybody—it is even true that he likes Bill." The same variable position and variable allegiance crops up at other points in the grammar: with negation in *I want not to go, I don't want to go,* with adjectives attached to certain noun phrases as in *I want a cup of hot coffee, I want a hot cup of coffee,* with tense in **I hope to shall see you, I shall hope to see you* (see Jespersen, *Modern English Grammar* IV, 7.2₈), etc. As a second illustration take the *with* phrase in the sentence
I always cut myself with a new blade.
It appears to be instrumental, and I am sure is felt as such, but since the order can be inverted.
With a new blade I always cut myself.
as in
With a new friend he always puts himself out.
which would be unacceptable if a pure instrumental were involved,

The underlying structure of phrasal verbs. Like other compounds, phrasal verbs may have diverse origins, in the generative-transformational sense of the term. Take the types that are intransitive in surface structure:

Transitive original via reflexive and deleted object:
He stood up the chair.
He stood up himself → He stood up.
Middle voice:
He piled up the things → Things piled up.
Deleted object:
He threw up his dinner → He threw up.
Basically intransitive:
It came up (in conversation).

These sources need to be studied with the same thoroughness that Marchand devotes to compounding in other areas.[7] Along with the generative question goes the semantic one of idiomaticity. In trying to assign a deep structure to *give up*, for example, we encounter other surface structures, one or more of which apparently ought to have the same deep structure as *give up*, yet differ slightly in meaning:

He gave up. (quit trying)
He gave up his money. (abandoned it)

---

*With a new blade he cut himself yesterday.
it appears that the *with* phrase is also functioning as part of a circumstantial complement: "When I use a new blade I always cut myself." If it is argued that in view of the inversion the circumstantial complement is the only one to be recognized (and that we are fooling ourselves in reading in an instrumental reading), the proof that both are there can be seen in the equivalence of the original sentence to
I always cut myself on a new blade.
—which means the same, and which cannot be inverted as the circumstantial *with* can:
*On a new blade I always cut myself.
7. See Hans Marchand, *The Categories and Types of Present-Day English Word Formation,* 2nd ed. (Munich, C. H. Beck, 1969).

Give up your friends if you must, but don't give up yourself.
(abandon yourself)
He gave himself up. (surrendered)
Idiomaticity of course is a monumental problem in its own right. At some points it seems that the facts are too refractory to do more than state them. My final example illustrates a curious intrusion of what almost appears to be an unconscious play on words:

Our program stands for the rights of the individual. (it occupies an upright position, like a milestone; stands foursquare)

We stand up for the rights of the individual. (we make ourselves conspicuous for, declare ourselves for)

He sticks up for the rights of the individual. (the foregoing plus stickiness: he declares for the rights and adheres to his position)

Index